SACRED SITES

Glastonbury

The Pocket Guide to

Your Magical Journey

Serene Conneeley

SACRED SITES: GLASTONBURY

First edition copyright © 2010 Serene Conneeley

All rights reserved. No part of this publication may be reproduced, stored in a retrieval system or transmitted in any form or by any means, electronic, mechanical, photocopying, recording or otherwise, without the prior written permission of the publisher.

Serene Conneeley
Series: Sacred Sites
Glastonbury – The Pocket Guide to Your Magical Journey
ISBN: 978-0-9805487-3-0

Published by Blessed Bee Books
PO Box 449, Newtown, NSW 2042 Australia
Website: www.SereneConneeley.com
Email: blessedbeebooks@yahoo.com.au

Cover: Daniella Spinetti
Photos: Serene Conneeley
Illustrations: Justin Sayers

"Travel is more than the seeing of sights;
It is a change that goes on, deep and permanent,
in the ideas of living."

Miriam Beard, American author and historian

"We travel, some of us forever,
to seek other states, other lives, other souls."

Anais Nin, French-Cuban author

"Twenty years from now you will be more disappointed by the things that you didn't do than by the ones that you did do.
So throw off the bowlines.
Sail away from the safe harbour.
Catch the trade winds in your sails.
Explore. Dream. Discover."

Mark Twain, 19th century American author

The magic of the earth

Since ancient times, sacred sites have had a powerful effect on people. Their vibrational essence, beauty, tranquillity and history, along with the magnetic power infused in each one by centuries of pilgrims steeping it with love and energy, can heal people physically, activate them spiritually and open their heart and their soul to their divine purpose.

Sacred sites are spiritually significant places that inspire the imagination and activate change and healing in those who spend time there. Each country has several places that are recognised as sacred, as do all religions and cultures, and visiting any one of them will be both a literal and a symbolic adventure, a journey to one of the most beautiful places on the planet as well as to the deepest, most sacred parts of your self.

Some are intricate manmade structures, such as the Inka city of Machu Picchu in Peru and the Pyramids of Egypt, while others are ancient paths of energy like the Camino, a pilgrimage across the north of Spain. Some are elaborately engineered stone circles such as Britain's Stonehenge, and others are natural formations like the Tor, the sacred hill in Glastonbury, England; Uluru, the huge monolith in Central Australia; and the volcanoes, mountains and waterfalls of Hawaii.

These are the seven I wrote about in *Seven Sacred Sites: Magical Journeys That Will Change Your Life*, a large book that has inspired many a magical journey, but which is too heavy to throw in your backpack and take with you on your adventure. And so here is the pocket guide to Glastonbury and Avalon, much smaller and lighter, with extra practical information squeezed in, and room at the end to add your own notes, and phone numbers and websites you'll need on your trip.

Like most sacred sites, Glastonbury is located on a series of leylines, invisible pathways in the earth through which currents of magnetic energy run, similar to the acupuncture meridians of the human body. Our meridians carry chi, life force, while the world's leylines channel the life force of the universe.

Also known as earth currents, holy lines and telluric tracks, leys have been described as the nervous system of the planet. They are routes of spiritual energy that have an intense, measurable power that activates growth and healing, and many people believe it's this powerful earth energy that makes sacred sites so transformational. Being on or near a leyline increases vitality, heightens awareness and amplifies spirituality and inner wisdom, because their energy is absorbed when you interact with them, either by walking along the lines or spending time at the sites they run beneath. This boosts physical health, increases psychic abilities and connects you to the life force of the planet. Plants grow better along leylines, animals thrive and the air itself sparkles with vivid energy and possibility.

The ancients were aware of leylines, and understood their purpose and how to attune themselves to and work with the energies. Early Christian monks felt the power of the leylines on some level too, and built churches and temples over existing pagan sites, often using the sacred stones in their construction, as is theorised with the church on top of Glastonbury Tor, which many believe replaced a circle of standing stones.

While the existence of leylines is disputed by some because they can't be seen, they are a universal concept, recognised by cultures that span the globe. Native Americans call them the spirit path, while the Australian Aboriginals have songlines and serpent tracks that link their sacred places. The Inkas of South America had a system of energy grids called ceques, and the art of geomancy known as feng shui is based on the Chinese belief in lung mei, dragon paths, lines of energy that flow through the earth and influence the fate of those who live along them, and thus the location of towns, placement of buildings and the arrangement of furniture.

In England two intertwining leys, the Michael and Mary lines, run directly from the southwest tip, at Saint Michael's Mount in Cornwall, to Norfolk, the most easterly point, passing through the country's most sacred places – including Boscawen-un, Burrowbridge Mump, Glastonbury and Avebury – on the way.

Dowsers identify these geomagnetic energies with divining rods, which I experienced within the inner circle of Stonehenge. As a leyline is crossed the rods swing dramatically, before stilling again once it's passed. Some people see this energy clairvoyantly, while others sense it as a physical sensation within the body or as a purely emotional recognition. In Britain in particular a new category of earth science is developing, which explores the power of leylines. Hamish Miller and Paul Broadhurst's book *The Sun and the Serpent* follows their adventures as they dowsed these leylines, and has a lot of information about the magic of the earth.

Glastonbury's power comes not only from the power of nature but also from the people who have lived and worshipped there for thousands of years. It is sacred to pagans and druids, who see the goddess in the landscape and have long been performing rituals in her honour, and are again today. It has significance to Christians, being the site of the first church built in England and an Abbey that was an influential ecclesiastical centre for hundreds of years. And it helps everyone see their own spiritual path more clearly, whatever that is and wherever it will take you. Being there will help you see the world with new eyes, allow the beauty and magic of this enchanted planet to open you up to your own truths, and nurture you as you discover the sacredness of your own deepest self.

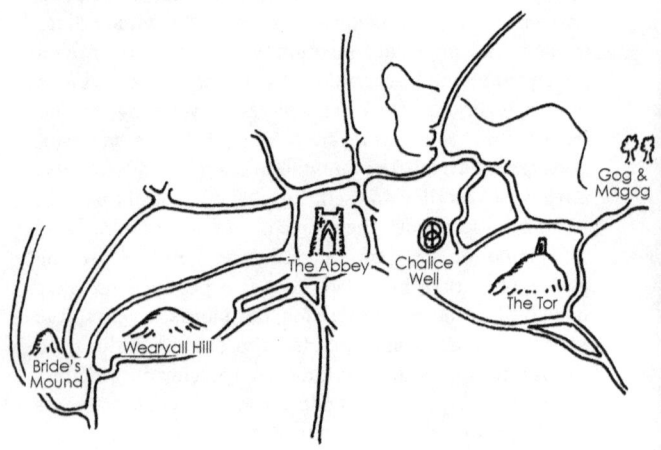

Unlock your inner priest or priestess

The sacred Isle of Avalon

Glastonbury, Somerset, England

Immerse yourself in the ancient magic of the priestesses and druids of the British Isles, attune yourself to the beating heart of the earth and its sacred energies, and hear the whisper of history in this mystical place where the early Christians worshipped, King Arthur lived valiantly, and the wise women made their potions.

The place

> "There is on the confines of western Britain a certain royal island, called in the ancient speech Glastonia, marked out by broad boundaries, girt round with waters rich in fish and with still-flowing rivers, fitted for many uses of human indigence, and dedicated to the most sacred of deities."
>
> *Saint Augustine of Canterbury,*
> *first Archbishop of Canterbury, seventh century CE*

Deep within the swirling mists of the ancient land of Britain is a tiny town of immense spiritual, religious and historical significance. Glastonbury, just a few hours southwest of London, England, has long been acknowledged as the spiritual heart of the country. It is a place of legend and myth that draws people of all faiths to wander the sacred earth and submerge themselves in a landscape that opens everyone up to the truth within their own heart.

Renowned as the mystical Isle of Avalon, it has been a place of magic and spirituality since ancient times. For centuries the priestesses did their healing work and followed the goddess here, druids worshipped alongside Christians before religion turned to war, and King Arthur and the chivalrous Knights of the Round Table constructed Camelot and defended the country from barbarian invaders.

Even today it is a melting pot of cultures, ideas and beliefs. In the last census it had the most residents of any town in the United Kingdom reporting "other religion", and pagans, Christians, Buddhists, Sufis, Hindus, New Age spiritual searchers and atheists all seem to happily co-exist in a community that fosters healing, growth and self-awareness, no matter what your spiritual path.

It was made famous in Marion Zimmer Bradley's enchanting bestseller *The Mists of Avalon* (and the telemovie, starring Julianna Margulies as Morgaine and Anjelica Huston as Vivianne, that was based on it), which details the pre-Christian goddess worship of the Old Religion and the real-life magic of the priestesses of Avalon. Through this and other legends, Glastonbury has touched the hearts of millions of people from around the world, while still managing to retain the quaint charm of a working farming village in the lush and gentle English countryside.

The town consists of just four main streets arranged in a square and surrounded by cute little cottages and shops filled with organic produce, tiny winding lanes lined with wild hedgerows, and fields of sheep and buttercups. Yet it has something for everyone tucked away behind the faded storefronts, within darkened stone churches and at the mystical places of nature for which it has become so popular.

Spiritual pilgrims today are drawn to the powerful energy of Glastonbury Tor, the massive green hill that towers over the town. It's been considered a holy place for millennia, and can be seen from miles away, an instantly recognisable piece of the sacred landscape, and a place where the veil between the worlds is thin.

Visitors climb straight to the top and marvel at the views and the strong, masculine energy of the hill, or weave their way to its centre by threading a path through the ancient seven-level labyrinth, a physical and metaphorical journey within. Believed to have once been crowned with a stone circle, and now holding the ruins of an old church tower on its top, the Tor is variously said to be a faery hill, a pathway to the underworld and Archangel Michael's mount.

Nestled at the base of the Tor is Chalice Well and its beautiful, peaceful gardens. This is where the priestesses did their seering, gazing into the sacred wellspring to divine the future, and where they drew the waters to concoct potions for physical and emotional healing. Today people still flock here to drink from the Red and White Springs, which have been credited with miracle healings, or submerge themselves in the pool to absorb the vibrational essences, as pilgrims seeking cures did centuries ago.

Chalice Well is also said to be the place where Jesus's great uncle Joseph of Arimathea took the chalice of the Last Supper, so it has special significance for Christians too.

Nearby, in an enchanted glade, are Gog and Magog, the magical oak trees that are the only two left of the ancient druidic processional avenue that once wound its way up the Tor, which provide a place of powerful, nurturing energy.

Across town, on the outskirts heading south, are the gentle slopes of Wearyall Hill where, according to legend, Joseph planted his staff and a sacred thorn tree grew. Across the road is Bride's Mound, a smaller hill next to a well that was dedicated first to the goddess Bridie and then to Saint Bridget, which is being reclaimed from the industrial area that had engulfed it, and is again a place of ceremony and spiritual reflection and meditation.

And in the centre of town are the ruins of Glastonbury Abbey, which is recorded as the first Christian church in England, and thus holds within its crumbling stones the history and beliefs of this two-thousand-year-old religion.

Throughout the beautiful grounds are tumbled down chapels, statues of saints and wooden crosses, the exposed foundations of tiny monks' cells, the intact old Abbot's Kitchen, tranquil lakes, apple orchards and herb gardens, and the graves of King Arthur and his queen Guinevere, whose story is a vital archetype and part of Britain's soul.

Glastonbury is a place of myth and magic, of history and legends come to life, but it is also a modern village where people live normal lives – farming, running their businesses, selling crystals, herbs, books or hardware, catering to tourists, going to school and church, commuting to London or working in one of the many cafes.

Here alternative spiritual beliefs flourish alongside more conventional ones – Christians converge on the town and its Abbey on holy days, there's a beautiful Goddess Temple where the new priestesses of Avalon undergo their apprenticeships, celebrate pagan festivals and hold open rituals for the community, as well as a number of churches, healing centres and even an ashram that encourages eastern meditation and yoga for those who stay there.

Whatever a person's faith, or lack thereof, Glastonbury is a sacred and timeless spiritual sanctuary that awakens the light within everyone who spends time there, and weaves itself into the heart and soul, healing and nurturing everyone who visits.

In addition to its significance through the ages and the reverence for the past it instils, which manifests in the form of goddess worship and other religious practices and rituals, Glastonbury also has a very modern effect. For even if its potent history is dismissed, the very land itself lives and breathes with a beautiful nurturing quality that embraces all who visit, regardless of beliefs or intent.

Walking through the quiet streets of this pretty village, up and down the gentle hills and through the beautiful gardens by the sacred wells and springs, your heart will reawaken because of the power that resides in the very earth here, and you will begin to see the magic within your own self as your inner priest or priestess is activated by your interaction with these incredible energies.

The present

> "Avalon is a landscape of the soul, a country of the heart. It's the land the poet and mystic see in visions, where the artist and musician find inspiration, and the soul goes for healing and spiritual refreshment. A timeless land that offers initiation and enlightenment to all those who embark upon the inner voyage."
>
> **Mara Freeman, British druid and author**

While people travel to the town of Glastonbury, for many it's the mystical dimension of Avalon that they seek. This is not a physical place but rather a state of being, a realm where you can access the inner world and your deepest intuitive self. Long ago, when the town was called Avalon, it was renowned as a centre of druidic initiation and knowledge. Women came from all over Europe to serve the goddess and train as priestesses, and people worshipped the Great Mother, practised the healing arts and communed with the divine on this sacred land.

It was a mystical place of enchantment and deep transformation, but when the new religion of Christ sent the Old Ways into the shadows, the wisdom was hidden away, so that now, reaching this magical realm has evolved into a vision quest of sorts. Not everyone who goes to Glastonbury reaches Avalon, or wants to. It is possible to walk through the town, have tea and scones in a cafe and climb to the top of the Tor without feeling the swirling air of magic and seeing the sparkling enchantment of this other world.

But many people have reported accessing this dimension. They have seen the light change and the atmosphere ripple before them, and felt the mists closing gently around them. Some experience Avalon descending as they sit in quiet contemplation by the sacred Well, while others stumble upon it as they walk along a wooded path as darkness falls and shadows lengthen. Some have crossed over into Avalon while walking the ancient labyrinth on the Tor, and others have gone there in dreams, bringing back wisdom to integrate into their waking life. Times of change – sunrise, sunset, midnight, as well as the turning points of the seasons – can make this magic easier to access.

Avalon is another dimension, a place between the worlds, but it also has a physical, geographical location, anchored on the slopes of the Tor and in the waters of Chalice Well. It is slightly removed, a kind of parallel universe that touches the seams of the real world yet floats apart, accessible to those with the eyes and heart to see. Avalon is where you can find answers and guidance, recharge your body and spirit and reawaken to the magic that is within you. It opens you up and reminds you there is more to life than the limited part that is seen. You can dare to dream, to live full out, to achieve your goals. You can reconnect to your own heart and soul, rediscover the beauty of the world and the potential you have to create your own perfect reality.

Avalon is a place you can reach no matter where you are in the world, because it is within you, a state of being where everything is possible and you are awash with magic and potential. But the easiest way to get there is by spending time in Glastonbury, visiting its sacred places and allowing yourself to absorb and be absorbed by the mystery and myth that permeates it.

The town lies in the shadow of the Tor, a beautiful grassy hill that mysteriously shapeshifts with distance and the changing light. While its outline can be spotted from other villages in the area, up close it seems to disappear. There are places in town where it and the ruined church tower on its top can't be seen at all, despite its hulking size.

Part of the Tor's mystery also comes from its shape – from some angles it looks like a symmetrical rounded hill, but from others it is completely different, almost rectangular in layout, with a narrow strip of land and a gentle slope from its base near Chalice Well, and an almost sheer drop on the other side. As the hill is climbed, the tower on the top also appears to move, sometimes looming high above before suddenly dropping below the summit, other times appearing to the left then later to the right. In photos it looks like a kid playing a trick, always in a different place, on a different level, yet from the top it's clear that the tower is located at the highest point.

The Tor, named for the Celtic word for hill, has been described as a magic mountain, the grail castle, a centre of goddess rituals, the land of the dead and a gateway to Annwn, the Otherworld, which was ruled over by the faery king Gwyn ap Nudd. It's also said that within the hill there are chambers, a crystal cave, the tomb and resting place of the great King Arthur, or even a hall of records holding ancient wisdom.

Walking up the pathways of the Tor to its summit is a spiritual experience in itself. One, the Pilgrim's Path, winds up the slope closest to town. It's a gentle approach, starting from the bottom of Wellhouse Lane near Chalice Well and climbing up past the place where esoteric author and spiritual teacher Dion Fortune lived and worked in the 1920s and 30s.

There is a bench halfway up so climbers can catch their breath and gaze out across the town to Wearyall Hill, then from there the path slopes slowly upwards to the tower at the top, which is approached with a sense of reverence and awe.

Another path rises steeply from the base at the other side. It's a shorter route, and was recently landscaped to better conserve the slopes and prevent erosion from the thousands of eager feet that climb this enchanted hill each year. The Tor is managed by England's National Trust, which has taken on the sacred charge of protecting the area while maintaining access for all who wish to visit.

Standing barefoot on top of the hill in the sunshine, gazing out over the beautiful countryside of flowers, patchwork meadows, ancient trees and quietly grazing cows and sheep, the power of the place is deeply felt. I've sat for hours on the grass here – in sunshine and rain, at sunrise, noon and sunset, in darkness and light, under the full moon and the dark moon – sensing the energy rise and fall.

I've had epiphanies about my self and my beliefs, realised the reasons for things that have happened in my life, let go of past hurts and embraced the future with a strength and positivity that owes much to the site and the energies it activates within.

Atop this sacred hill I could feel a tangible force, a vibration that quickens the heart, the spirit and the soul. It is the life force of the earth, which pours forth so strongly on the Tor's grassy slopes. Part of this energy is from the impact of the Michael and Mary leylines that run through the hill, two powerful lines of earth energy that race upwards and intersect on the summit in a swirling vortex of power and a melding of masculine and feminine energy.

Leylines amplify feelings, experiences and emotions – love and the quest for enlightenment, but also fear, anger and bitterness – and that can be painful unless you're aware of it and ready to face the things within you, the weaknesses we all have.

A local guide who took me to nearby Cadbury Castle, the reputed location of Camelot, said Glastonbury is a hard place to live because it brings up a lot of stuff within, issues from the past and present, and not everybody is ready to deal with that. The worst fights he's ever had have been on the Tor, because its energies amplify everything – positive and negative, good and bad.

Conflicts of the heart and self are played out here, and the mysteries of love, hate, death and rebirth are revealed. Glastonbury itself means Isle of Glass, and residents say that living here is like being in a place where your thoughts and emotions are constantly reflected back to you. And you'd definitely have to be ready for that!

It is up on the Tor that I have most strongly felt Avalon surround me, as I sat watching the legendary mists roll in. As the sun sets and the shadows lengthen, as the cold settles in place over the warmth of the day, a thick, swirling cloud creeps into the hollows of the town, between the hills and over the fields, wreathing its way around houses and through the Abbey ruins, drowning trees, animals and buildings as it rises and spreads out over the land.

Referred to as the Lake of Wonder and the White Lady, this mystical phenomenon covers all the lower ground, and only the grassy hills – the Tor, Chalice Hill, Wearyall Hill and Bride's Mound – remain above the tide line. Coloured by the last rays of the sun, and later by the rising moon, the mist is an ethereal, enchanted substance, holding secrets within each molecule. Breathing it in can change you, can transport you, can transform you. People hear whispers in this mist – the voice of the goddess, of the faeries, of your own inner knowing. It speaks to you of things you always knew but had forgotten, putting you back in touch with your soul and opening you up to hear the voice of your heart.

Another way to access the dimension of Avalon is to walk the old labyrinth carved in the side of the Tor. While debate continues over the exact purpose of its construction, whether or not it was intended as a sacred pathway doesn't really matter – it is one today because we have made it so. Spiritual pilgrims from around the world walk the spiral path to the Eggstone, the psychic centre of the labyrinth, and back out as a meditation and a transformational step in their own spiritual development, a modern-day initiatory experience or rite of passage. It is an amazing process, a sacred ritual that you can do alone or with a group of people with the same intent.

For various reasons I didn't end up making this pilgrimage until my fifth visit to Glastonbury. Perhaps I wasn't ready until then. Maybe I had to attune myself to the energies of the Tor to prepare myself. But finally I tied a red ribbon around my wrist, symbol of the goddess Ariadne who oversees such journeys, and walked the ancient path that winds around and around the Tor and back in on itself, into the heart of the hill and the other dimension of Avalon. I followed the labyrinth into my heart, my self, my desires, my needs, my limits. I moved through the mists of my mind, and through the veil that separates the real world from the Otherworld that lies over Glastonbury.

It is a beautiful, meditative walk, through sweetly fragrant apple orchards and a lush, magical wood on the lower slopes, then along the steepest sides at the top, where it's hard to get a foothold and you have to cling to the almost vertical slopes with your hands, fingers clawing into the earth.

Each of the seven levels is linked to an element, an emotion and a chakra, which activate as you walk, opening you up to the universe and your own inner wisdom. You can feel the spiritual footprints of the pilgrims who trod this track before you, and reach out for the lessons and knowledge they accessed, which now lie within this etheric path around the Tor.

You'll be touched by the history floating around, and will feel the wisdom of the priestesses, or the saints, or even Arthur and his companions, brush against you as you make your journey. It takes several hours each way, between four and eight depending on how you walk it, how often you pause to connect to the land and what you need to get out of it. It's suggested that you make your way inwards one day then walk out another, psychically holding yourself within the centre of the labyrinth while you physically return to the base of the Tor down the ordinary path, then going back to the centre another day to wind your way out.

This allows the wisdom you acquire and the realisations that occur to sink deeper into your soul, penetrating all layers of your psyche. You should also pay special attention to your dreams on the nights in between, when your spirit self remains at the centre of the labyrinth, because secrets will unfold and answers will be revealed to you.

And so a few days after I wound my way inwards I walked back outwards – away from my past and towards my future, towards my true self. I felt lighter, transformed, having let go of my fears and the things that had scarred me, the things that no longer matter. Recently engaged, I walked towards my forthcoming marriage, but for everyone it is a personal journey, a way to deal with the past, prepare for the future, answer a question or learn to listen to your inner guidance.

Another aspect of the Tor's powerful impact is the spiritual emanation of thousands of years of worship and ritual that have taken place atop this grassy knoll. Everything seems possible up here, as you feel the heartbeat of the planet and hear the whisper of the spirit. And it affects people from all over the world, who follow all kinds of spiritual and religious paths. I've spoken to Christians, pagans and atheists up on the summit, and all felt something uplifting and inspiring them. Some call it God, some goddess, some believe it is nature or science, and others simply soak it up and are grateful for the experience.

> **"Sacred wells and springs form a centre of healing and ritual, dedicated to the deities or saints of the religion of the dominant culture, but still the waters from the Mother's womb. They have attracted worship and been sacred to many religions because of the powerful earth energies that converged at the spot, making Otherworldly connections easier."**
>
> ***Cassandra Eason, Celtic witch, teacher and author***

At the foot of the Tor is Chalice Well and its beautiful gardens and water features. For millennia it's been an important source of healing and spiritual power to all those who have lived in the area, no matter what their beliefs. Pagans saw it as the goddess Ceridwen's cauldron of knowledge and revered its healing powers, while for Christians it became the chalice of the Last Supper, placed there by Joseph of Arimathea. Both interpretations are symbolic of the holy grail and enlightenment, and encapsulate a form of healing that transcends just the physical and works on the emotional and spiritual levels as well.

Natural springs and wells have long been revered both for their life-giving water and as a source of spiritual power and magic, as places where the veil between the worlds is thin and communication with the gods and goddesses of the nature religions and with other dimensions can be made.

They're regarded as gateways to the spirit world, and throughout time they have been used to divine the future, cast spells, send messages and act as a metaphoric mirror to the soul.

Chalice Well is all these things, but most importantly it's a place of healing. In ancient times the local priestesses used the vibrational power of the water to treat the sick, in baths, medicines and as the water itself, and today it is still renowned for easing pain, curing illness and treating emotional and spiritual malaise. Modern pilgrims have also claimed cures for everything from migraines and kidney disorders to chest infections and depression.

Miracles of healing attributed to the waters of Chalice Well have been documented for centuries. In 1582 John Dee, the Elizabethan mathematician and alchemist, claimed to have found the elixir vitae – the elixir of life and immortality – at the Well. And while he did eventually die, it wasn't until he was in his eighties, a grand old age in those days.

In 1750 a man dreamed that if he drank the water every Sunday for seven weeks he would be alleviated of his life-long asthma. He followed his vision and claimed at the end that he was cured, as did many of the thousands of people who poured in to the town in the hope of their own healing.

Glastonbury was a famous spa town throughout the 18th century, when people would travel great distances to take the waters, drinking from the spring as well as submerging themselves in the Pilgrim's Bath in the gardens near the Well. A pamphlet of the day, called *The Virtues and Efficacies of the Waters of Glastonbury*, records dramatic healings from rheumatism, deafness, "most difficult and troublesome respiration", ulcers, tuberculosis, paralysis and leprosy.

There was also a Pump House in Magdalene Street, opposite the Abbey, an earlier version of current spa resorts, where people went to bathe in and drink of the water that was pumped there from the Well.

Today many of the healings seem to be on a more subtle but deeper level. The water is full of iron and other minerals, but that's not what causes the healings – a multivitamin could do that. Instead there is a vibratory force that is released and activated when the spring water comes to the surface from deep within the earth and interacts with the elements of air and light above. This water is also infused with the energy of the leylines that run through Chalice Well Gardens, and the magic of this extraordinary place.

Experiments have found that the water from holy wells is lighter than normal water. And while this effect is not yet understood, pilgrims continue to visit the Well for healing and spiritual transformation, knowing that it works and unconcerned by its cause.

Chalice Well is fed by the Red Spring that pours forth from under Chalice Hill, the gentle mound that rises in the shadow of the Tor. The water is a constant 11°C and has a red tint and a metallic taste due to its high iron content, caused by ferrous oxides oxygenating as the water reaches the surface. Across the lane outside the gardens is the White Spring, which is fed from a source deep within the Tor. Unlike the iron-rich water of the chalybeate Red Spring, this water is calciferous, with a high calcium carbonate content.

The Red Spring is considered to be for physical healing, while the White Spring imparts a spiritual quality, so a mix of the two is recommended to create physical and emotional wellbeing. Only a small amount is required – a few drops of each in a glass of tap water imparts benefits, and too much can be a little unsettling on the tummy. The two springs also represent the alchemical melding of male and female energies to create wisdom and life force, with the White Spring representing the masculine and the Red or Blood Spring representing the feminine.

Prehistoric tribes drank from the Red Spring at least five thousand years ago, and the Well has been in constant use since long before the time of Christ. It pumps out a constant 112,000 litres a day and has never failed or run dry, even when the whole country was in drought, and there have been a few times when Chalice Well was the town's only water source.

Long ago a stone well shaft was built over the spring. Some date it to around 1200CE, but the remains of a two-thousand-year-old yew tree which was part of a processional way to the Well have been dug up, and Iron Age shards and Roman pottery have been found around it, indicating that it could be far older. Connected to the well shaft is a stone chamber that is illuminated by a beam of light at sunrise on the summer solstice, which also points to ancient origins.

Once the well shaft stood above the ground like a more traditional well, but since then the surrounding area has been built up with earth, and the well head is now at ground level, covered by a beautiful lid bearing the vesica piscis symbol, designed by Hamish Miller, and surrounded by overhanging trees, flowers, stones and steps where people sit to meditate near the source. The vesica piscis is the ancient sacred geometric pattern of two interlocking circles, which symbolises the merging of the conscious and the unconscious, the physical and the spiritual, yin and yang, god and goddess, and the inner and outer worlds.

Today the Well is surrounded by the enchanted realm of Chalice Well Gardens, and a small entry fee is charged to help maintain the beautiful space. In 1912 educational pioneer Alice Buckton bought the Well and the land around it, which at that time was the site of a Catholic monastery, and held it in spiritual trust for the people of the area. She created a college and guest house there, produced mystery plays, wrote visionary poetry, performed rituals with other locals – Dion Fortune, Frederick Bligh Bond and the famed Avalonians of the early 20th century – and allowed access to the place for spiritual contemplation.

After her death Wellesley Tudor Pole, a spiritualist who instigated the Silent Minute during World War II, formed the Chalice Well Trust and bought the Well and the adjacent house to prevent it being used for industrial purposes. The Trust has managed the gardens and grounds ever since, maintaining the magic and intent of the place and ensuring it will remain a sacred site accessible to the public for all time.

Walking up the cobblestone path under a canopy of flowers to the entrance and stepping through the gateway is like entering another world. You feel a sense of reverence like being in a church, yet this is an outdoor shrine, a place of nature and the goddess. When I first spent time in the gardens I was flooded by a great sense of homecoming. It was as though I had lived here before, and understood the deeper purpose and the subtle vibrations of the place.

Sitting quietly at the Well and gazing into the dark waters under the ancient yew trees, I had a vision of the long-ago priestesses in their long robes, gathering water for their healing potions, strewing herbs on the surface as they watched images of the future unfold before their eyes, making blessings and respecting the ancient water element and its power.

The air shimmered and my skin tingled. Had I been here before, with them? Everything felt so familiar, so much a part of my very being. My heart expanded as I felt their energy and intent merge with mine. I sensed their devotion to their healing work, which connected us across the centuries, and an inner peace and tranquillity that I longed to reconnect with. I also felt washed clean by the energy of the place and the sense of gentle nurturing that permeates the air.

Another beautiful place to absorb these vibrations is at the lower pool, located near the garden's entrance and shop, which has been built in the shape of the vesica piscis. This pool is fed by a goddess-shaped water feature that has been stained red by the iron-rich waters, which have long been associated with the life-giving blood of the earth mother and the fertility of the planet, the goddess and women.

This feminine aspect of the site was lost for centuries when the Christians claimed it for their own, insisting the waters ran red because Joseph hid the chalice of the Last Supper there, overlaying the old symbolism of the place with their own new meaning. They adopted the vesica piscis as their own, using its sacred geometry when they designed their cathedrals.

They also took the shape made by the intersecting circles – the fish shape they called an ichthys – as their symbol, yet again it was appropriated from a nature worship thousands of years older than theirs, as evidenced by the ancient cave paintings and carvings of goddess figures and yoni sculptures found around the world in the same form.

On the way up to the Well is the Lion's Head Fountain, where the water can be drunk as it pours forth through the carved mouth. There is a soft green lawn and a sweetly scented, colourful garden surrounding the fountain, so you can sit where the water spills out, meditating in the sunshine, absorbing the warmth and comfort of the dancing sunbeams and drinking deeply of the healing liquid.

Down some stone steps is King Arthur's Courtyard, a shady, walled garden area where the water cascades down in a crystal clear waterfall to fill the Pilgrim's Bath, the place people have come for centuries to submerge themselves in the healing waters. This is where the Michael and Mary leylines intersect again, after previously meeting in the Abbey grounds and then later winding up and around the Tor to connect on the summit, so it is a powerful place of swirling energy.

The first time I walked through the archway into this quiet area it touched my heart in a way I'd never felt before. I sat at the bottom of the waterfall under the shade of a giant tree, being splashed by the sparkling spray of water and gazing at the tiny flickering candles, flowers and ribbons left here as offerings, and cried. They were happy tears, tears that seemed to wash away years of pain and bitterness.

I felt my heart opening – a physical sensation, not just a metaphor for an emotion. I was shaking and a little off-balance, moved by the power of the place and mesmerised by the misty spray and the lush, vivid green. I felt linked to this ancient source of healing in a way I couldn't really comprehend or explain, but could deeply feel.

Later the sunshine peeked through the leaves overhead as I sat with my feet and hands in the healing waters of the Pilgrim's Bath and soaked up the peace and mystical air. It's so quiet here – people only speak in hushed tones, if at all, and the water spilling down into the pool sounds so tranquil and calming.

Suddenly I felt such a jolt of connection and recognition. I don't know whether it was because I'd once lived a life here as a priestess of Avalon, whether it was the energy of the leylines that activated such deep emotions within me, or something else altogether, but it doesn't really matter. I felt healed, renewed, awakened and somehow lighter, transformed by the beauty and power of this site.

This was also where I met a man from Holland who had come to give thanks for the extraordinary healing he'd received from Chalice Well. He'd been in hospital, dying, when a friend showed him photos of the garden and the spring. Somehow the energy of the place healed him, and he had come as soon as he was well enough to experience its power for himself, express his gratitude and drink the waters. Many others have also reported distant healing, showing that you don't even have to visit the place physically to connect with its energies.

There are other magical places in the gardens too. There's a peaceful area near the Well called the Sanctuary, a small courtyard garden where two small springs meet in a tiny pool and statues gaze tranquilly down. The Meadow is a beautiful grassy area overlooking the whole complex, where people picnic and chat, and the Cress Field is the place where the Guardians light the Beltane bonfire, and where I've taken part in a few pagan ceremonies over the years to mark the seasons and the ancient Wheel of the Year.

And rising above it all is Chalice Hill, from where the Well's water emerges. It's a beautiful, gentle mound of grass and sunshine, which is dwarfed in size by the nearby Tor, but has its own power and majesty.

Those who lived and worshipped in this place thousands of years ago would be so happy with the way the Well and the gardens have been protected, maintained and celebrated. There's not a single spiritual cliche here, just respectful and magical guardianship of a place that will hopefully remain preserved in this manner for centuries to come.

The Trust also operates a retreat house and lodge within the grounds, with accommodation for Companions. This provides 24-hour access to the Well and the gardens, and is one of the most beautiful experiences in Glastonbury. It's truly magical to drink the water under the silvery light of the full moon, or to wander through the enchanted realm in the pre-dawn mist, hours before the gardens open to the public, watching tiny squirrels scamper along the grass and butterflies float above the healing pools. And sitting alone at the Well when everyone has gone for the day, while the golden light of sunset illuminates the grounds, makes the sense of peace and healing complete – it's truly a balm for the soul.

But even when the grounds are closed there is constant access to the vibrationally charged water from both the Red and White Springs on Wellhouse Lane, near the bottom of the path up to the Tor. On the outside wall of the gardens is an outlet for the Red Spring water, and across the road there's one for the White Spring, trickling out from a semi-abandoned building, where locals fill massive containers.

Once there was a pretty wooded valley between the Tor and Chalice Hill, and their two springs emerged side by side from the earth so the energies of the waters could mix freely. Now however a road and a reservoir separate them. There is a conservation group trying to restore the old setting and reawaken old rituals there, but until that happens it is people who continue to create the alchemy of blending the energies from both springs as they imbibe the healing waters. Some drink only one or the other, but most combine the powers of the Red and the White Spring waters to receive the full range of healing.

"People have long gone to sit beneath the mighty oak to gain strength and spiritual renewal. The outside world can be forgotten and the inner world can slip back into perspective. The oak can help you find new understanding and vision, gained from your experiences, and bring strength and courage to face your life. The oak tree's mighty presence helps restore faith in yourself."

Glennie Kindred, English artist, writer and pagan celebrant

Another beautiful, spiritual place to spend time is in the shade of Gog and Magog, the last two remaining oaks of a long-ago processional way that led to the top of the Tor. The druids trod this path two millennia ago, when their ways and their reverence for nature were respected. Gazing at these massive old trees, silent sentinels over so many centuries, I could understand why these ancient people spoke of shifts in perception as they walked beneath the branches.

I could picture them moving quietly through the darkness in solemn candlelit procession, the full moon shining down, long robes swishing around their bare feet, the priestesses with blue crescents emblazoned on their foreheads, and overhead the leafy arches of an avenue of sacred oaks.

It's a long, steep walk from the base of the Tor, down a beautiful country lane and across an old-fashioned country stile, to reach these two trees, which are suffering the vagaries of time, sometimes appearing dead or at least in a long sleep. It's been said that they alternate energy, and that usually only one is covered in foliage while the other remains bare, and then they swap, taking it in turns to receive and be nurtured, the way a relationship should be.

Traditionally such avenues of sacred trees consisted of pairs, and each alternated feminine and masculine energies. Thus Gog and Magog are deemed a couple, and attributed with personalities and human characteristics. Perhaps this is why people are so outraged that in 1906 a farmer chopped down the long pathway of ancient oaks to clear the ground for cattle, leaving these two Oaks of Avalon as the only reminder of what once was.

They have been dated to around two thousand years old, and are so wide that it would take several people holding hands to reach around their trunks. One of their now-gone friends was almost four metres in diameter and had more than two thousand rings when it was felled, reinforcing the druidic wisdom that the oak is king of the forest.

Gog and Magog stood alone for a century, but recently the Glastonbury Conservation Society replanted a line of oak trees to commemorate the old processional way. This is another thing I love about the town – people respect nature and the past and want to preserve it. The group is involved in many conservation projects in the area, such as improving pathways to prevent erosion and planting more than forty thousand trees in and around the town. They've also nominated Glastonbury for a place on UNESCO's list of World Heritage Sites in order to better preserve the cultural and natural significance of the place.

The countryside of England was once covered in forests of ancient oak trees. They were sacred to the pagan tribes, representing strength, endurance, wisdom and courage. Druids performed their rituals and ceremonies within a grove of oaks, and wands made from the wood helped magical practitioners get in touch with their inner power and symbolised protection, strength and fertility.

Medicinally, a decoction of oak bark was used to ease congestion, improve muscle tone and heal infections, the leaves were used to stop bleeding and decrease inflammation, and a homeopathic remedy eased stress, aided relaxation and controlled cravings – and many practitioners still use these methods today.

Oaks were also associated with the crowning of kings and the preaching of gospels, and were the meeting places where laws were proclaimed. They marked boundary lines and processional routes, people got married and performed other ceremonies beneath the leafy branches, and it was thought that energy, wisdom and calm could be absorbed from the tree by leaning back against its trunk.

It's certainly very peaceful sitting in the shade of these two oaks, which are entwined with tangled rose bushes and wild berries. It feels like a place of faeries and magic, where time can stretch and your perception can shift. Gog and Magog are hollow in parts, with caverns, nooks and burrows at the roots – possible houses for creatures of all kinds. Offerings hang from the branches and nestle in the cracks, including crystals, ribbons, bells, incense, jewellery and water brought from Chalice Well to nourish their roots.

They're also surrounded by honeysuckle and wild nettles, which sting with a long-lasting, bitter ache. Like many things in nature however, the antidote grows right next to it – the leaves of the dock plant ease the pain of the nettles. The druids and priestesses who worshipped the old oaks understood nature, and believed that the earth always provides a cure to anything toxic that it creates.

On the way back to town I walked up through the field of buttercups where the processional route once ran. There's so much energy on this ancient path – I could really feel it seeping into my body and my being, a tangible, potent sensation. There is old magic soaked in the ground here, imprinted on the ether, as there is at many of the places in Glastonbury, which have gained power over the centuries through the varied but constant worship of the landscape and the deities that once ruled it.

Another sacred tree is the holy thorn that first grew on Wearyall Hill, another beautiful mound to the southwest of the Tor. Legend has it that when Joseph of Arimathea returned to Glastonbury to found his church he stuck his wooden staff in the top of the hill, where it took root and sprouted into a living hawthorn tree – which was apparently a fairly common event in the lives of the saints.

Whether you believe this legend or not, there is something miraculous about this particular plant and its descendants, which flower twice a year – once in spring, as all hawthorns do, and then again in winter, around Christmas, which many perceive as a Christian miracle (or, for the more pagan of outlook, a message from the goddess of this land).

No one has been able to explain how this occurs, but attempts to make it happen to unrelated trees or grow one from seed always fail – it's only the trees grown from a cutting of the original that flower twice a year. There are a few of these holy thorns in the town – the windswept one on Wearyall Hill, as well as those in the grounds of the Abbey, in Chalice Well Gardens, outside Saint John's Church and on Magdalene Street – all grown from cuttings from Joseph's tree.

The original thorn tree was reportedly chopped down and burned by Oliver Cromwell's troops during the English civil war of the 1600s, which was ironic given that the Christians this tree meant so much to had done the same thing to the sacred groves of the druids when they forced their religion on them.

In pre-Christian times the hawthorn was also a sacred tree, the symbol of springtime and fertility, and was believed to have special powers of transformation. Its white flowers were used to boost circulation and improve heart health, its red berries to relieve stress and anxiety, and an infusion to aid kidney health and long life. Magically it was used for good luck and protection, and was connected to the faeries.

"Glastonbury has always been a centre of pilgrimage. Although the Goddess is here in the land, people of all faiths come because this is a spiritual centre for all. There's something very powerful in the energy of the place itself that draws people."

Kathy Jones, priestess of Avalon, teacher and author

For all the magic and history of Glastonbury and Avalon, these days it's best known to most people as a three-day music festival, which is actually held on a farm 10 kilometres east, in the village of Pilton. It began in 1970, when Marc Bolan headlined, and throughout the years acts as diverse as David Bowie, The Cure, Boomtown Rats, REM, Hole, White Stripes, Coldplay and Robbie Williams have appeared.

In the hippie spirit of the area the festival is environmentally friendly, with recycling and camping facilities, and millions of dollars have been raised over the years for charities such as Greenpeace and Oxfam. I've never been to it, although I've been in the town while it was on, but each time I plan a trip to Glastonbury I'm asked if that's why I'm going.

For spiritual seekers it is instead the earth energy, the sacred landscape and the transformational powers of the Tor, the Well and the Abbey ruins that make Glastonbury a place of pilgrimage. And unlike many sacred and magical places, it's fairly easy to visit. While crossing the mists to Avalon involves a much deeper quest, it isn't hard to physically reach Glastonbury.

From London you can catch a bus or hire a car to make the 220 kilometre journey. The gentle slopes of the Tor and its crumbling tower can be seen from several towns away, acting as a beacon to draw visitors nearer, teasing as it seems to change direction and shape as the road twists and turns.

I still vividly recall the first moment I laid eyes on it, as I travelled there by bus, the sky bright summer blue and the hill a deep green, and the most recent time, trying desperately to arrive in my little car before dark, the tower lit up by the rays of the approaching sunset, melding dramatically with a black storm cloud as autumn turned the whole world golden.

Considering the size of the town, there are a surprising number of places to stay, from camping sites and the friendly hostel located in the 16th century coaching inn on Market Place to the luxurious George & Pilgrims Hotel just a few doors up, which was originally built for pilgrims to the Abbey and is reputed to be haunted by various old souls.

There are also many B&Bs to choose from, as well as several self-catering places, an ashram with budget accommodation and the Chalice Well Gardens retreat house, which includes 24-hour access to the Well. To stay here you must join the Trust, which includes free entry to the Well, regular newsletters and discounts in the shop, and which supports the organisation in the important work of preserving this ancient site.

All the sacred places are easy to find and within walking distance of the town centre, but there are also a few tour companies that offer half-day, full-day and week-long journeys into Glastonbury's Arthurian, druidic and Christian past, which can help you delve beneath the physical level of the town and unlock the secrets within its heart.

And there are many healers, both traditional and New Age, spiritual courses and workshops, as well as public gatherings, rituals and special events that take place throughout the year.

In addition there is a Goddess Temple, the first one in Britain for fifteen hundred years. Co-founded and run by pagan author Kathy Jones, it is a beautiful space which people are welcome to visit so they can meditate, soak up the divine energies of the goddess, get in tune with nature and the sacred landscape, and meet like-minded souls.

Kathy also trains modern-day priestesses of Avalon, who undergo a three-year apprenticeship and initiation into the traditions of old, studying to reclaim the role of healers and keepers of wisdom who celebrate the cycles of life and nature. They conduct beautiful open rituals on the solstices, equinoxes and pagan cross-quarter days, and at the different phases of the moon.

They also provide healing circles and oracle sessions, and the individual priestesses (and priests) facilitate marriage blessings, naming ceremonies and divorce rituals, provide midwife services, offer correspondence courses and are pagan prison chaplains, amongst other things, as well as co-ordinating the annual Goddess Conference, a five-day celebration filled with workshops, artwork, performances, rituals and healing.

They have created a beautiful temple space above a shop in a courtyard along the High Street, as well as a goddess hall on Benedict Street, bought in 2008 from fundraising efforts in order to hold workshops, trainings and larger ceremonies in a place befitting their spiritual purpose.

The past

> "Once upon a time Glastonbury was under the sea, but a stirring of geological forces pushed the Tor above the surface. For a while it looked out over empty water, then the sea-bed heaved itself up and became Somerset."
>
> **Geoffrey Ashe, British historian and author**

Long ago the land where Glastonbury is located, which lies near the Bristol Channel leading into the Atlantic Ocean, was one of the few sections of solid ground in the Somerset region, an island among the flooded lowlands that have since been drained and built upon.

For thousands of years the area was inhabited by Neolithic tribes, and others before them, island-dwelling people who lived in harmony with the land, worshipped the sun, the moon and the trees as sacred and took part in rituals to honour the seasons and the landscape.

Legends persist that the earliest dwellers in Glastonbury were survivors from the lost land of Atlantis. Whether or not this is true, there is archaeological evidence of settlement in the area from at least 4000BCE, long before the druids were there. At this time the formerly flooded areas had begun to silt up, and islands had emerged amongst the marshland. A stone axe head, a goddess figurine and elaborate wooden trackways through the bogs have been found from this period, preserved in layers of peat, which provide hints of a people who worshipped the Great Mother goddess common in Europe at the time.

Later the Celts started settling in the area, building hill forts on high ground and maintaining ties with Brittany in France – a place of forests and stone circles that to this day shares stories of Merlin, Morgen la Fey and King Arthur with Glastonbury. The town was known as Avalon, and it was a centre of druidic and priestess initiation where a series of nature-based gods and goddesses were revered.

Historians can't agree on the exact origins of the word, but Avalon comes either from the name of the god Avallach or Annwn, who ruled the underworld said to reside within the Tor, or from the Celtic word for apples, the sacred fruit that grows in the orchards of the town.

Apples are symbolic of soul transformation, regeneration and immortality, thus relating to the underworld, and the apple tree was considered the Celtic tree of life. The fruit was given to the kings of Britain to symbolise their marriage to the land, which was the embodiment of the goddess. Later the Christians referred to the town as Ynis Witrin, the Isle of Glass, which developed into Glastonbury.

As Avalon it was the realm of earth mysteries, the Lady of the Lake and the deities that are still associated with Glastonbury today – the maiden Bridie, a goddess of healing and inspiration who became hidden within the legend of Saint Bridget; the nurturing mother goddesses Modron and Rhiannon, who were associated with fertility, protection and manifestation; and the crone goddess Ceridwen, keeper of the cauldron of knowledge, transformation and rebirth.

There are also legends of the Nine Morgens, the guardians of the secrets of Avalon who are said to still be present in the landscape, and who taught the priestesses the arts and sciences, including herbal lore, astronomy, prophecy, healing and music.

The most famous of them is Morgen la Fey, who became entwined in the myths of ancient Britain, claimed as King Arthur's sister-lover and also known as Morgaine and Morgan. She is a "dark" goddess, keeper of the deep mysteries, divination and initiation, and the shadow side of Guinevere, the "light" goddess embodied in the land and the sunshine of spring.

In 1892 some of the complex lake villages – tiny manmade islands that were constructed in the watery marshlands – of the goddess-worshipping Avalonians were uncovered near Glastonbury, providing a fascinating glimpse into their life and beliefs. The system of spirituality they followed revered nature and preserved the environment, and their deities were a part of the sacred landscape. They believed the planet was alive, and that they had been entrusted to keep the balance and harmony of nature. In turn the earth nurtured, fed and balanced them.

Their religion embraced tolerance, equality and the right of all people to worship in their own way. Men and women were equally respected, and they believed in a masculine and feminine face of the divine, with a priest and priestess presiding over rituals and learning – which brought them into conflict with later dogmas.

When the Romans invaded Britain in 43CE they brought their "one true God", and killed those who would not convert to their ways. They also built an incredible network of roads across the country and drained huge tracts of land, yet Glastonbury and its surrounds remained prone to flooding from the nearby ocean, and even up to 1000CE continuous work had to be done to protect the area from the sea and keep it drained. Much of this labour was performed by the monks of Glastonbury Abbey, and the 10th century abbot Dunstan, who later became a saint, was particularly renowned for his efforts.

For a long time the Tor was one of the few pieces of land to have emerged from the waters, a green and fertile island amongst the sea of lakes. And today it remains the most significant landmark in the region, with the present-day town built in its shadow, on ground that was once underwater.

This gently curved natural hill is 158 metres high and more than twice as long, and is shaped like a teardrop, with a rounded main section that draws out to a longer, narrower part on the side closest to the town. It's comprised of layers of clay and limestone, with a harder sandstone top that has weathered erosion well. The iron-rich waters of its underground spring have also assisted its stability, as deposits of iron oxide from the water have strengthened the soil. There are strange egg-shaped boulders in the sandstone, called by some omphalos stones, as well as calcite crystals deeper within the hill.

"Saint Michael shrines are commonly set on high places, where beacon fires once blazed on the days of the festivals. The tower of Saint Michael on the Tor is one of the stations in an alignment of Michael shrines that extends along the spine of southwest England that corresponds to the path by which, according to legend, Christ once proceeded from Cornwall to Glastonbury."

John Michell, English philosopher, archaeoastronomer and author

While there's evidence of a fifth or sixth century hill fort on the Tor, attributed to Melwas, a rival of King Arthur, today it is the tall stone building that remains on top, visible from miles away, that ignites people's imaginations. This 14th century church tower is all that is left of the medieval monastery of Saint Michael, which was built on the ruins of earlier places of worship. Church records indicate that there was a very early church and monastic settlement on top of the Tor, built by Saint Patrick – although archaeological evidence reveals that the first probably wasn't constructed until the 10th century, many years after his time.

This centre was dedicated to Saint Michael, who was known as the slayer of dragons to represent the Christian repression of the Old Religion that had flourished at the site previously. Pagans were symbolised as dragons and snakes by the church, thus when Saint Patrick drove the snakes out of Ireland, he was forcing the followers of the Old Ways to flee or risk being killed for their beliefs.

Building a church dedicated to the dragon slayer atop the Tor, which was sacred to those who worshipped the goddess, was a way for the Christians to publicly stamp their mark on the area and discourage alternative spiritual practices. Why else would they have built a church at the summit of this very steep hill – which parishioners would have hated to climb, especially in winter – when the beautiful Abbey in the town below was well used and easily accessible?

In 1275 an earthquake destroyed Saint Michael's church, which some attributed to the vengeful ancient spirits of the land, although science has explained that the cause of the instability was the caverns within the Tor. A new, smaller church was rebuilt on the site, which lasted until 1539, when this building, except for the tower, was destroyed during the Dissolution of the Monasteries, the four-year period when Henry VIII decided that the monasteries, and the monks, owned too much land. He closed them all down, seizing their wealth, selling off their land and destroying religious shrines and churches across the country.

Today the tower adds another dimension of reverence and focus to the natural hill. Its shape is the perfect symbol of the male energy of the Tor, which contrasts with the feminine energy of Chalice Well in an alchemical marriage. And on a more mundane level it provides welcome shelter from the bitterly cold winds that howl around the top.

Winding around the Tor to the summit is the labyrinth that was carved in the side of the hill more than five thousand years ago. Labyrinths are common to all cultures, and evidence of them has been found on archaeological digs all over the world. The Tor labyrinth was a processional way related to the old goddess worship, an initiation rite symbolising the journey through life, death and rebirth, and was walked in order to communicate with the deities of the time.

Many believe it was created by the same people who built the great astronomical observatories of nearby Stonehenge and Avebury, and that it was the centre of a series of visual markers such as hills and rivers that provided sight lines so they could observe celestial events and determine seasonal midpoints and days of lunar significance, acting as an ancient calendar. There was once a stone circle atop the Tor that was part of this observatory, and an alignment of standing stones that ran down the hillside, although only a few of the latter remain.

One of the popular legends that surrounds the Tor is that King Arthur and his Knights of the Round Table rest in eternal sleep within it, and will awaken when England is in its hour of greatest need. Another states that the Tor itself is their metaphorical round table, and that around it are a series of landmarks shaped by hills, waterways, roads and earthworks that correspond not only to the signs of the zodiac but also to each of Arthur's twelve loyal knights.

In this story the warriors had to go to each landmark in turn and complete a quest or an initiation – whether it was to literally slay a dragon or save a damsel in distress, or was a more esoteric mission in which they had to learn a spiritual lesson, depends on how literally the tale is interpreted. After successfully completing each task they would ascend the Tor through the labyrinth to attempt the final challenge.

Galahad, the son of Lancelot, is thought to have been the only one to succeed, because of his spiritual purity. He reached the top and was rewarded with the holy grail – which is said to have caused him to leave his mortal body and go into the light. For the holy grail of legend was not an object but a state of enlightenment and self-knowledge, a quest that people still visit Glastonbury today in an effort to fulfil.

It is in fact believed that King Arthur, or a real-life man he was based on, did live in this area and unite the British people against the Saxon invaders after the Romans departed England in the fifth century. Such a leader did have a stronghold at nearby Cadbury Castle – thought to be the site of Camelot – and there is evidence of his presence at the hill fort that existed on the Tor during this era. This was a time when goddess worship still echoed through the forests, Christianity was still establishing itself and Roman morals and codes of behaviour held influence – the chivalry that defined this period of history.

Arthur trod a difficult path in trying to reconcile the Old Ways with the new, in adopting the current religious order without betraying his people, who still saw a feminine aspect of the divine. And with his death in battle the old wisdom went underground, lost to the world and yet still energetically present in the sacred landscape of Glastonbury.

Perhaps this is why the town is emerging now as a centre of goddess worship, as the secrets of the past, of the idea of divinity being a combination of masculine and feminine, a power that is within each and every one of us, is revealed from the earth itself.

"Glastonbury Abbey is like a man struck down in his prime. The spirit of the Abbey is there, alive and energising. We have only to close our eyes to feel the atmosphere of a great church all about us. There is spiritual power there. Standing in the great nave, looking towards the high altar, we feel the movement of life."

Dion Fortune, British occultist, psychic and author

For those who prefer their religion more mainstream, the ruins of Glastonbury Abbey are renowned as the site of the first Christian church in the British Isles and the birthplace of Christianity in the country. While the pagans and New Age seekers have the Tor and Chalice Well, the Christians have the Abbey ruins, which to this day are a place of pilgrimage for believers from all over the world.

Each week services are held in the small Saint Patrick's Chapel, which was built in 1500CE and is still intact, or outside in the remains of the great medieval Lady Chapel. There are also annual summer pilgrimages to the Abbey, both an Anglican and a Catholic one, which draw people from as far away as Australia and the US.

Visitors of all faiths can wander through the sprawling, grass-covered grounds – which include the stunning ruins of early chapels, grand altars, monks' dormitories and shrines, the still-whole Abbot's Kitchen building, an apple orchard, a sweetly scented medicinal herb garden and a duck pond – to soak up the energy and feel the power of the religious worship that's taken place here over the centuries.

Church records report that Joseph of Arimathea built a wattle and daub church dedicated to Mother Mary, said by some to be his niece, on land given to him by the druids. When he arrived in Glastonbury after the Crucifixion, reputedly with the chalice of the Last Supper, the druids accepted him as a man of great learning. Legend has it that they discussed religion and theology with him, and all learned from each other and respected each other's different paths to the one divine truth. Sadly though this tolerance didn't last, and later Christians persecuted the druids, priestesses and followers of the Old Ways.

According to 12th century historian William of Malmesbury, Joseph came to Glastonbury from the Holy Land with eleven others around 63CE to start their religious foundation and spread the word of Jesus.

The burned remains of their church allegedly still exist below the later constructions that made up the Abbey, and from that time onwards a community of monks lived and worshipped there.

This new religion slowly grew, continuing alongside the old in relative harmony until Roman emperor Constantine legalised Christianity in the early fourth century. He was trying to promote tolerance, because until then followers of Christ had been denied the right to practise their beliefs, but it was the death knell for the goddess religions of the country, and created a new form of bigotry.

Missionaries swept through Britain zealously preaching the scriptures, and by the end of the century paganism was illegal and the priests and priestesses of the Old Ways were killed or driven out, their sacred groves torn down and their worship outlawed.

Christianity became the official religion, and Glastonbury turned from a place of druidic wisdom to a centre of monastic glory. The popular Irish saints Patrick and Bridget both spent time in the area. Patrick arrived around 445, and declared Glastonbury "the holiest earth in England", a claim still repeated today. There are even stories that after his mission in Ireland was complete the snake-banishing cleric returned to England, gathered together the hermits of Glastonbury and became the first abbot. He's said to have been buried at the high altar – although there is some debate over whether this was the famous Patrick or another missionary of the same name.

The holy woman Bridget also visited from Ireland, in 488. She prayed at the chapel dedicated to Mary Magdalene at Beckery, on the outskirts of town atop Bride's Mound, which later became Saint Bridget's church in her honour. But before any religious buildings ever existed here, the hill had been a small island sacred to Bridie, one of the primary goddesses of the Celtic world. Its well had also long been dedicated to her, but it was renamed in honour of the saint, a common occurrence in the British Isles as the known world became Christianised.

Bride's Mound had been the gateway to Avalon, and a women's community existed there in both pagan and Christian times. Today goddess ceremonies take place once more on this hill, and there is a chapel in town dedicated to Bridget as both saint and goddess.

In 712 the first stone church was built in the grounds of the Abbey, which successive abbots extended, increasing the religious power of the town. In the 10th century the influential monk and court adviser Dunstan arrived in Glastonbury. He became abbot in 945, and in his lifetime he instituted Benedictine (Catholic) rule, helped the Abbey recover from the Saxon sackings, constructed sea walls to protect the town from flooding, enlarged the church and built new cloisters.

He later became Archbishop of Canterbury, the highest religious office in the land, attracting further glory to the town, and he also remained abbot of Glastonbury until his death in 988. In *The Domesday Book* of 1086, it was recorded that Glastonbury Abbey was the richest monastery in the country, and many religious men who later became saints, including David, Augustine, Collen, Paulinus, Patrick and Benignus, lived and served there for a time.

In 1184 a fire destroyed the whole complex and many of its treasures, but within a few years it had become a pilgrimage site again due to the discovery of King Arthur's bones in the cemetery, another connection that joins people of all faiths. In 1191 monks found two skeletons they claimed were Arthur and his wife Guinevere's, buried under a stone slab with a lead cross that said, in Latin: "Here lies buried the renowned King Arthur in the Isle of Avalon."

The bones were kept in the chapel for almost a century, then placed in caskets and reinterred in a black marble tomb before the high altar in a ceremony attended by King Edward I and Queen Eleanor. Pilgrimages to the site of their burial became even more popular, which has led many to question whether the monks really did find any bones, and if they were in fact those of the former monarch, or whether the claims were simply a publicity stunt to draw pilgrims back after the fire.

Interestingly, the reburial of the husband and wife together, close to the point where the Mary and Michael leylines intersect, symbolises the marriage of masculine and feminine energies, another pagan concept embraced by the priests. In Glastonbury there are three energy vortexes created by the intersection of these leylines – beneath the ruins of Saint Michael's Church up on the Tor, within the Chalice Well Gardens, and at the site of Lady Chapel in the Abbey grounds.

The druids established their healing centres, initiation places and ceremonial sites at the places where leylines intersected in order to harness and make use of the amplified energy, and the monks followed their lead, perhaps unconsciously, by building Lady Chapel on the same site. Today people of all faiths feel a power there that is beyond religion, something older and deeper and more profound.

In addition, beneath the ruins of this chapel is a small dark well surrounded by ancient stones. It was once sacred to the goddess, used by the druids and priestesses for ritual and healing, and was later dedicated to Mary and Joseph, adding to the multi-dimensional power of the place. Today visitors breathe this in by spending time in quiet contemplation on this spot, finding their own sense of meaning and interpretation in this historic place.

After the fire's terrible destruction, the Abbey was

slowly rebuilt. The new Great Church was consecrated on Christmas Day 1213, renewing the glory of the Abbey and making it second only to London's mighty Westminster in size, wealth and influence. The kings and queens of England often visited the area and attended services in the chapels, and the abbots wielded immense power and lived in total luxury.

This all came to an abrupt end during the Dissolution of the Monasteries. King Henry VIII stripped eight hundred religious orders of their wealth, land and churches, claiming them for his own, and forcibly converted the country from Catholicism to the new Church of England. His actions were partly due to greed and partly so he could get a divorce, which was forbidden by the Catholic church of the day.

In 1539, Glastonbury Abbey was the last to be closed. Abbot Stephen Whiting, who had long supported the king, was pronounced a traitor when he refused to join the new faith and hand over all the Abbey's treasures, and he was hanged, drawn and quartered up on the Tor as part of a terrible, senseless persecution and abuse of royal power.

Afterwards the Abbey grounds were vandalised. Arthur's tomb went missing, although the monks created another grave nearby which can be visited today. It doesn't look that impressive, just a rectangle of grass bricked off with a sign above it announcing it as the resting place of the brave king, but it is rich with symbolism, legend and history.

Glastonbury Abbey was slowly disbanded then, and the stones were taken away to build houses, much like the way the early church had pulled down the Neolithic stone circles to construct their places of worship. It was a tragic end to one of the most powerful religious institutions in Europe, which had controlled vast lands, possessed a great library and been regarded as England's most sacred place.

King Edmund had been buried in the Abbey in 967, in 1125 it was so famous that William of Malmesbury wrote a history of it, *De Antiquitate Glastonie Ecclesie*, and 18th century English writer William Blake's famous poem *And Did Those Feet in Ancient Time*, which became the hymn *Jerusalem*, was written about Glastonbury and the legend that Joseph had taken Jesus there as a young boy.

After the dissolution, the Abbey ruins remained deserted for more than three hundred and fifty years, until in 1907 the Bath and Wells Diocesan Trust bought the site for the Church of England – a sad irony for many Catholics – and started to restore and study what was left.

Between 1908 and 1922 archaeologist Frederick William Bligh, a friend of Dion Fortune's, discovered the foundations of many old chapels and monks' cells that had been built over or buried underground, and helped reconstruct what the Abbey looked like when it was one of the most magnificent in the country. Sadly he was fired when he revealed that much of his information was channelled from a monk who had lived at the Abbey hundreds of years previously, yet his work was instrumental in restoring and rediscovering its history.

Like most of Glastonbury, the Abbey incorporates the influence of different faiths, with geomantic experts claiming the building was designed on similar mathematical principles to Stonehenge and the Pyramids, and it having been constructed along the leylines that run through the town.

Today the fascinating museum just inside the entrance to the complex features a model of what it looked like in the 1500s, and presents a history of the site through all its incarnations, with stories of how the monks and abbots lived through the ages, their beliefs and challenges, the progress of this holy community and all the legends associated with it. There are also

Living History characters who wander through the grounds in summer, offering unique insight into the lives of those who worked at the Abbey centuries ago.

Wandering through the ruins, which are charmingly picturesque against the vivid blue sky and lush green grass of the grounds, I could envision how it must have looked in its heyday, with its soaring arches and grand construction. I walked through parts of Lady Chapel, which is open to the sky but still retains some walls and a sense of the grandeur it once had. Also known as Saint Mary's Chapel and dedicated to Mother Mary, it was built on the site of Joseph's primitive church, which was also dedicated to her.

Beneath it in the crypt is Saint Joseph's Chapel, created in the 1500s, which features an altar where services are sometimes conducted today. Other Abbey buildings are not quite as intact – some are simply foundation stones that have been dug up from the earth, some are single walls – but there is something very stirring and romantic about the old stones and the broken arches of those that still stand.

Cooing white doves nest in the ruins, and huge black ravens also swoop through the air, adding to the impression of duality, of yin and yang, of balance. There is an air of peace and tranquillity throughout the complex, and I felt that I'd stepped back in, or outside of, time. Flowers bloom, spreading a sweetness that lifts the heart, and I was blanketed by an atmosphere I could physically feel, that muffled the sound of the street outside and soothed the soul.

After a long and dramatic history, these ruins remain a beautiful, holy site. The whole of the Abbey grounds are a place of power, and while I don't follow the Christian path, I've walked through here many times and felt the echo of the beliefs that have been celebrated in this spot over the centuries and the combined energy the place still holds.

The purpose

> "If I was obliged to leave Glastonbury tomorrow I would always remember the sense of a gateway that it gave me: a gateway to infinite possibilities, not abstract but right here on earth. It gives me the sense of a place set apart – a place quite other than the mundane – where I can be all I can be."
>
> *Nicholas Mann, British anthropologist and author*

Glastonbury has a glorious past, myths interweaving with facts to create a rich tapestry of spirituality and history. But while people continue to debate whether it was Joseph who built the first Christian church here, if Arthur really lived and the presence of the goddess within the green hills, the most important thing is that it has the ability to transform people now. All the stories are beautiful and have deep meaning, and whether they are literal retellings of history or just symbolic parables doesn't diminish their effectiveness or power.

The sacred waters of Chalice Well heal, be it Ceridwen's cauldron of inspiration and immortality, the chalice of the Last Supper or a vibrational energy that will soon be measurable and understandable. The energy of the Tor opens your heart to your own deeper truths, whether it was once topped by a druidic centre, a monastic settlement or a ring of stones. Perhaps these are all simply reworkings and reinterpretations of the same archetype anyway, transformed as people change, beliefs evolve and time moves forward.

Whatever your faith, visiting Glastonbury and spending time breathing in its sacred beauty will unlock the deepest parts of your true self. Many people find physical healing here, especially in the gardens of the Chalice Well, while others experience a blossoming of their spirit and a new understanding of their own innate power. Walking in the footsteps of the people of old also activates new wisdom and knowledge, and helps you recognise the priest or priestess that lies within you, the god or goddess that is your true self – a part of you, not something separate and outside of you.

For many people Glastonbury is a place of nurturing goddess energy and gentle healing power. Thousands of years ago the inhabitants worshipped the Great Mother, the spiritual embodiment of the physical planet, and today she is still revealed in the landscape of the town. The waters of the Red and White Springs are seen as her life-giving nourishment. Topographical maps of the hills and valleys of the area reveal the shape of the Mother Goddess lying on her back, her head and shoulders etched from Stonedown Hill, with Wearyall Hill as her straightened left leg, Windmill Hill her bent right leg, the Tor her left breast and Chalice Hill her pregnant tummy.

From a different angle there is another goddess shape, the crone Ceridwen flying across the town on Bridie's swan, with Wearyall Hill as the swan's outstretched neck and head, and the old woman represented by Stonedown Hill as her hunched over back, Windmill Hill her stooped head, Chalice Hill her breasts and the Tor her once-fertile womb.

The Great Goddess was considered the giver of life, the eternal mother, the source of all things, and in ancient times women were worshipped as a manifestation of her because of their ability to create and nurture life. Today the goddess-centred worship of much of the spiritual belief in Glastonbury reflects this, empowering women to follow their own hearts and decide their own path.

In the 1970s there was a thriving feminist consciousness in the town, and while its spirit remains, it has become more inclusive since then, helping both men and women find a balance between the masculine and feminine energies of their own being and learning to understand themselves through a connection with nature and the seasonal cycles of life, the earth and the divine.

In venerating the goddess in her triple aspect of maiden, mother and crone, as they did in the past and they do again now in the Goddess Temple in Glastonbury, there is also renewed respect for older women, which will hopefully radiate outwards and change perceptions. Celebrating all the cycles and ages of life changes the emphasis in our throwaway society. While in times gone by elders were held in high regard and their advice respectfully sought, in much of the western world today, from Hollywood down, older women are discarded and their wisdom ignored, while older men run companies, countries and the church.

Yet in the pagan community and worldview all people are valued and age is a badge of honour, a mark of experience and wisdom. Recognising and valuing the crone, in both a literal form and as the energy of the wise man or woman inside that everyone can access, is an important part of the energy of Glastonbury today, and the purpose of the place for many. Being here teaches you to value all people, including yourself, nurtures your individual strengths, and encourages you to explore your own path and understand what is important to you.

It also unlocks your potential and allows you to see yourself as you could be – whole, complete, with all your dreams fulfilled. It's like being in another dimension where limits don't apply. It's a place of transformation, and if you're ready to let go of the restrictions and the repressed parts of your inner self that are holding you back, the gentle energy of the place will nurture you through the healing process.

It also helps crystallise your own beliefs, and understand what's in your heart, rather than what you absorbed from your upbringing, schooling, society or friends. In Glastonbury a religious or spiritual path is a way of life rather than a system of thought and dogma, and people here come to their own conclusions through personal experiences and transformative realisations rather than rote learning.

Some say this is because of its location as the heart chakra of the world, and that the energy of the town has always been more conducive to new thought and harmony of religious expression than most.

It has been – and continues to be – the gateway of so many changes in spiritual beliefs. It was a place of goddess worship for thousands of years, the centre of druidic initiation and teachings for a millennium more, and then the birthplace of Christianity in the British Isles. And perhaps it's no accident that so many atheists are now writing books and challenging accepted worldviews in nearby Oxford, representing the birth of a new era of scientific thought.

"The spiritual power of Glastonbury changes lives. It is a natural sanctuary where the earth spirit is teacher. It comes alive in the landscape, in the peculiar shades of light, the changing seasons, the air we breathe. When people come, their intent is to live the spiritual values of caring, sharing and living lightly on the land."

Frances Howard-Gordon, local film director, author and publisher

Regardless of world events, Glastonbury is one of my favourite places as much because of what it represents to me as for the beauty and peacefulness of the town and its special sites. It has been the mirror that reflected my inner heart back to me, the place I found a name for what I believe and a connection to all I hold sacred. Over the years it has nurtured my self-reflection, activated growth and new awareness in me and held me safe as I explored my inner world.

The first time I stayed there and immersed myself in the sacred energies, I had just been to Peru. I was touched by the spirituality of the people there, and respected their history and beliefs, but their sense of deity and method of worship wasn't mine.

In the wilds of the Amazon jungles I had seen flashes of gentle green hills and ancient wells, and had visions of standing within a circle of stones, arms open to the sky, gentle sunshine caressing my face. In the meditation we did in the Temple of the Condor at Machu Picchu I kept hearing a name that sounded like Sheridan, which made no sense to the people I was with or the place I was in.

But when I walked the sacred landscape of Avalon I knew I had come home. The gentleness of nature soothed my soul, and I found peace and healing by the Chalice Well and in the sunshine, mists and clouds up on the Tor. Breathing in the energy of this land energised and inspired me, and the light and the atmosphere felt so familiar.

I went to a talk held by the Pagan Federation in a bookstore in town. As I randomly opened a book while waiting for people to arrive, Sheridan was revealed as Ceridwen, the goddess of knowledge and rebirth, and I knew this was the name that had been whispered to me in the mountains of Peru. Ceridwen is a Celtic deity, symbolic of the feminine principle, of wisdom and of crone energy. Some believe Chalice Well is her cauldron of inspiration, and that those who drink from it are changed forever, even if they don't realise it at the time. I know I was.

As the talk began, I was excited to hear the articulation of the beliefs I'd always held dear. Here, on the other side of the world to where I live, the inner truths I'd always felt in my heart and mind were being expressed. I experienced a deep feeling of belonging amongst these people who also felt the magic of nature, and discovered a sense of home on the sacred hills and by the holy wells of this place.

On my way into town that night there had been a baby snake on the footpath – symbol of wisdom and healing – showing me the way forward. As I walked back to my B&B later, mind spinning, a sweet little black cat leaped out in front of me and rubbed against my legs, purring, making me smile. My pagan heart was awakening.

The following night was the full moon, and I decided to celebrate it by basking in its silvery light up on the Tor, an initiation of sorts into my own deeper magic. I knew that it would become full at 4.15am, so half an hour before that, after a few hours spent excitedly tossing and turning in my narrow bed, I quietly slipped on some warm layers of clothing and crept outside, feeling like a kid sneaking out of home. I started to wind my way reverently around the ancient peak, tracing the path of the priestesses on their ceremonial processions to the top.

In awe, I felt myself absorbing the spiritual energy and wisdom of those who had lived and worshipped here before. The fact that the clouds still covered the entire sky like a dark blanket didn't bother me – I just mouthed a silent prayer to the universe and expressed gratitude for my journey. Soon I left the path and climbed straight up the steep side. At times I had to cling to the grassy hillside with my fingers and toes, stumbling in the blackness, smiling, filled with wonder at the magic of the moment and the beauty of the night.

Finally I stood on the summit, slightly breathless and shivering a little in the breeze. At the moment the moon became perfectly full I gazed up at the sky, and suddenly the clouds parted and I was bathed in silver light. I felt a power rush through me, and felt a thrill of excitement that the moon had showed itself to me in that instant. This connection to nature is the basis of the earth magic that has long been practised here, and that is becoming popular again today.

The moon has been worshipped as a deity for thousands of years by people throughout all countries and cultures, with its phases echoing the maiden-mother-crone aspects of the goddess. The moon controls the tides of the oceans, the cycles of the human body as well as the emotions, and stimulates magical experiences, divination skills and the ability to go within and access the deepest intuition.

I stayed up on the Tor for hours, thinking, dreaming, meditating, staring at the sky, feeling a connection with this ancient land and the sense of the mystical feminine that is embodied in the gentle landscape and beauty of nature. I revelled in the strength and wisdom imparted by the dancing moonbeams, then gazed in wonder as the sun began to snake fingers of colour across the opposite horizon.

It was truly breathtaking – the moon peeking out from behind the clouds just for me (or so I liked to think!), the sky gradually lightening, and the approaching dawn painting the heavens in vivid pinks, golds, oranges and purples. I thought about the stories of the grail quest, of Galahad finding enlightenment and self-knowledge, and as I sat alone on the Tor in the misty dawn, I felt close to an illumination of my own self, my own soul, and that I was beginning to find answers to my own quest.

"It is our collective and individual responsibility to preserve and tend to the environment in which we all live. This planet is our home. Taking care of our planet is just like taking care of our own home. Our very lives depend on this earth, our environment."

The Dalai Lama, Buddhist monk, exiled Tibetan leader and Nobel Peace Prize winner

Walking the sacred landscape of this pretty corner of England reminds me to be in tune with and aware of nature, and to slow down and breathe in the energy and wisdom of the earth, which is available to all of us on this incredible planet if we want to open up to it.

Like Machu Picchu, Glastonbury is a place where all the elements come together in a magical way. The healing waters of the Well, the mystical air around the top of the Tor, the sacred earth of Chalice and Wearyall Hills, and the fiery power of the sunshine and the inner flame of the Tor all meld together, an alchemical blending of the four elements. Absorbing them reawakens the ideals I held dear as a teenager, before work and rent and commitments got in the way – looking after the earth, seeing the trees, rocks, animals and air as sacred, fighting against nuclear bases, fundraising for peace and an end to poverty.

The earth supports and nurtures us, and we have a responsibility to treat it with respect and care, and not exploit the resources that sustain us. Some modern-day pagans believe in the literal existence of gods and goddesses and deities within the landscape, while others simply revere the beauty and power of nature and the complexity and immensity of the universe. But whatever their world view, they all feel a deep connection to the earth, and to environmental issues as a result of that. They hold the planet as sacred, and express their spiritual beliefs through protecting the land, conserving resources, campaigning for change, utilising organic agriculture and produce, and creating a new environmental awareness.

The most precious example I saw of someone connecting to the old wisdom of Avalon, and the thing that moved me the most, was not an elaborate pagan rite or glamorous ceremony. It was a man on the Tor the day after the spring equinox celebrations, picking up all the rubbish left by the spiritual revellers. I was shocked and disappointed to see all the cigarette butts, food scraps and empty bottles left so carelessly on this holy ground, so I asked him for a plastic bag and spent the morning helping him clear up the earth.

Paganism and magic isn't just about dancing naked around the fire (although that has its place for some!). It's about revering nature, assisting the earth, and connecting with it. Doing what you can for people and the world. That day I reclaimed my environmental consciousness and the activism of my idealistic youth. I went to an internet cafe and rejoined Greenpeace, adding my voice to their campaigns and determined to remember this feeling when I got home.

It made me so sad that people could desecrate such a sacred site. They went there to celebrate the vibrant new energy of spring because of the spirituality of the place, the natural beauty and strong earth energy, the ebb and flow and tides of life you can feel pulsating within the Tor, then destroyed what they love about it.

But hopefully the essence of the place will have got through on some level to those who recognised its significance but had such little respect for it, and will help them grow, and become more aware of themselves and the earth. Glastonbury is a gentle, patient teacher, ready to aid anyone who opens their heart to listen.

I've been to the town several times now, at different times of the pagan year so that I could celebrate nature with like-minded people who dance on this sacred earth with the same joy as me. I've leaped the Beltane fires alone and with new friends and dear ones. I've burned my intentions and longings in a fiery cauldron like a spell, and felt the magic unfolding. I've whispered prayers into a candle sent to float on the vesica piscis pool with everyone else's hopes and dreams.

Each time I learned something more about myself, and about the world. I let go of something I no longer needed, and started to see myself more fully as the person I can truly be, filled with love and light and all the energy of the universe.

One summer solstice I found myself trapped on the Tor by the mists of Avalon, and it was so beautiful. I'd climbed the hill on solstice eve to soak up the magic of the sunset, then gone down to Chalice Well for a Midsummer Night's Eve ritual. The gardens were all lit up with coloured candles, faery lights and incense, creating an enchanted, mystical land. There was a Buddhist chant at the Well, theatrical performances, songs and harp playing, and people of all faiths joined together to meditate on what they wanted to manifest in the coming year.

Then just before midnight I threaded my way back up the path to the Tor in the darkness. I found a little spot among the drummers, didgeridoo players, singers and silent watchers, and settled in for the night. By 2am I was freezing cold, having loaned my scarf to a girl with fewer layers on than me, and decided to go back down and snuggle up in bed for a few hours before returning to watch the sun rise.

But by then the famous mists of Avalon had stolen quietly in, and the Tor was surrounded by the thickest, whitest, most magical substance. It was like the densest clouds I'd ever seen, so thick and white and full of form, but shifting and dancing and recreating itself too. It seemed as though it was alive, enfolding all of us, and the whole experience was so surreal. Suddenly it was like I really was on a tiny island and was trapped there, unable to get back down and across the lake to solid ground, or reality.

It is these mists that have added to the magical legend of the town, this memory of Avalon and the dimension of knowledge and wisdom that can be accessed by slipping through this veil, which is so thin here. The usual landmarks – Gog and Magog, Wearyall Hill, the church towers in town, my B&B – had all drowned beneath the mist. If it wasn't for the flickering outline of the tower on top of the Tor I wouldn't have even known in which direction anything was. And there was no way I could get down now without becoming lost in the mists, wandering off the path or falling off the Tor, so I sat there and shivered, smiling, dreaming, until colour began to stain the horizon and we all stared in anticipation.

And then everyone was awake and vibrant, calling out salutes to the sun and the solar god as solstice morning unfolded and Midsummer Day came to life. It was 3.30am, and still incredibly cold despite it being the middle of summer, but all of a sudden there was so much hope and optimism around me. The sun took ninety minutes to rise, but it was beautiful – the slowest, most gentle sunrise I've ever seen, and it painted the mists too, spreading out in soft pinks and golds and warm lavenders and mauves.

Finally it rose fully above the horizon in all its fiery, fierce and golden splendour, warming my heart, lifting people's spirits, filling us all with joy and touching the world with its sense of radiance.

The summer solstice, known as Litha, represents rebirth and light in the sacred Wheel of the Year, in both an archetypal and literal sense. The day is about acknowledging and celebrating your achievements and setting new goals, and also recognising what isn't working in your life and letting go of negative things, or purifying them to make them positive. I've done a lot of that in Glastonbury over the years, on so many levels. Somehow the powerful earth energy helps activate this change, while gently nurturing you as you grow.

"What greater thing is there for two human souls than to feel that they are joined... to strengthen each other... to be one with each other in silent unspeakable memories."

George Eliot, 19th century English novelist

My most magical, mysterious and illuminating experience happened on one of my most recent visits to Glastonbury, when I broke through the mists and wandered for hours in the magical state of being that is Avalon. I went there for my honeymoon, to finally share my special place with my beloved, and the whole time we were there we felt the most blissful state of sacred union, my inner heart melding with his and filling me with a sense of self so strong that I will be able to hold on to it forever.

Night had already fallen by the time we'd driven down from London and found our little cottage, but we had a sudden sense of urgency to go exploring. So we walked hand in hand up the High Street in the gathering darkness, all jetlag falling away as we passed the looming Abbey ruins and the peaceful beauty of Chalice Well Gardens. It was spookily dark as we turned in to the ivy-clad, tree-lined laneway that leads up to the Tor, but we stumbled our way up the stairs to the gateway, clinging together, and stepped out onto the lower slopes of the mystical hill.

Suddenly everything changed. It was like we'd stepped through a gateway and into another world, into the mists, although we didn't know it at the time. Slowly and steadily we climbed the hulking peak. I felt the steepness and paused for breath, but he didn't.

The next day when we walked up it again my beloved was surprised by how hard the climb is, but on this night he strode effortlessly ahead, with a sense of urgency that compelled him to dart upwards as fast as he could to face what was at the top. A few times he asked if I'd seen the flashes, but I hadn't. Nor did I see the same apocalyptic sky he did, or hear the voice telling him that he was going up the Tor to die.

Instead I saw a building in the sky to the left of the tower. Many people have reported seeing things there – visions of stone circles, places of learning, monks' cells, old temples, crystalline structures. It felt like a clue to what was going to come next, or perhaps to the mystery of who we had been to each other in a past life, or what had drawn us to this tiny town in this ancient land now.

When we finally got to the top we realised we were blissfully alone. We stared into each other's eyes forever, and his face kept changing, as mine must have too, because sometimes he looked at me as though he didn't know who I was. For a moment two other people took us over. Or were they us too? The us we once were? The us we are becoming?

Whatever it was, something very deep and ancient was being played out between us. It was intense, and surreal, a moment outside of time and meaning. As we held hands on the summit I heard a whisper in the wind: "You've chosen well. This is a love beyond time, outside of time, throughout time." And then more mysterious words: "He was the Keeper of the Well, and now he will keep your love safe."

As I struggled to comprehend what was being said, and who or what could be saying it, my new husband was getting messages and being bombarded by feelings too. At one point he looked deeply into my soul and said, so solemnly: "Now we really are married." And it was true. At that moment we knew our vows were consecrated, in a way they hadn't been when we'd spoken them in front of our celebrant, and our union became more real, more sacred.

Standing there together, holding on to each other, in a space between the worlds, was beyond words, beyond understanding. Vows were exchanged, and something deep shifted between us, grew, bonded. The final part of our wedding took place here, as we stood together alone on a magical hilltop across the world, where it seemed we had been together before, even though in this life at least we hadn't.

The darkness was so thick and close – although for my beloved the sky was all aflame, fiery red and shifting, while mine was a deep velvety blue and speckled with twinkling stars – yet we could see each other perfectly. There was such overwhelming urgency and passion between us, the most sacred feeling of deepest love and connection. Heart to heart, god to goddess. Just holding each other close, or gently kissing, was a kind of magic, an initiation into the sacred mysteries of life and love.

And then, at the same instant, we understood that it was complete. We suddenly felt chilled by the freezing wind, and knew it was time to descend our faery hill, shivering as we clung together to walk back down the Tor, and back into the world.

Before we departed, as we passed through the tower, I felt a presence that seemed to have been there the whole time. It was a supportive, protective, feminine energy. Not a physical one, because we were alone there, but something beyond. She was crouched in the corner of the tower as we left, and I thanked her as we passed, without knowing what or who it was.

For my beloved it was a masculine presence up there, as though God himself was communicating with him, and a dreamscape that had long haunted his night visions. He felt that something within him died up there atop the Tor, and that he had been reborn in some way. On this mystical hill all the subtle pieces of the magical puzzle that is our connection came together so profoundly, and we understood that it was the spirit of Avalon rather than the priestess in New York who had actually married us.

I don't know what happened that night, or how we passed through the mists and into Avalon. We can't explain or define it, but there was a definite magic that we tapped in to together in this enchanted town, a universal force of love and connection, and the tiny web-like threads of it still swirl around us wherever we are in the world.

Scientists may not be able to measure Avalon yet, or prove it exists, and there isn't a rational explanation for its power, but there's no doubt that people do have extraordinary experiences there, experiences that change them forever. Some go back in time to heal their past, others find pieces of their future selves to weave into their consciousness, and some access another dimension of themselves, or the world, to become more fully realised.

Perhaps one day the reason that transformation occurs so readily in this location will be understood, but until then Avalon remains alive, thriving in the physical realm where Christian and pagan still live alongside each other, balancing the masculine and feminine, the god and the goddess, in each pilgrim who journeys there, and being held safe in the in-between dimension that can be accessed in dreams and visions, meditation and art, and absorbed by those who walk these beautiful hills and streets.

The next day we spent hours together in the Chalice Well Gardens, marvelling at the carefully tended flower beds, the ancient twisted trees, the peaceful well head dressed with roses, ivy and tiny candles, the healing Pilgrim's Bath and vesica piscis pool. As we sat in the shaded courtyard by the waterfall, birds chirping around our head and hopping between our feet, each look into each other's eyes seemed to be another vow, a deepening of our bond, another step through time.

We heard voices again, more messages about keepers of wells and hearts, and we felt as though we belonged there, or had been there together before. And in all the photos we took by the Well and throughout the gardens we look different, ourselves yet somehow Other, as though the light we felt inside could manifest physically and be captured on film.

There had been serendipitous moments involving this place as we'd prepared to marry. The chalice we bought for the ceremony was from there. And when we spoke to our American celebrant she said she didn't know if we'd heard of a town called Glastonbury, but she had some water from its sacred spring that she felt guided to use in our vows.

As we ran our hands through that same water now, we refilled the chalice and drank again from the same cup, creating a new ritual. We breathed in the air scented with roses from the offerings, and felt the spirit of this place course through us, opening our hearts to the eternal truth of who we really are.

As I gazed at my beloved I saw the god within him, the beauty of all that he is and the potential of everything he can be. And as I smiled into his eyes, I saw there the reflection of the goddess essence within me, and the qualities of mine that he recognised, but which I had always refused to see.

That is the gift of Glastonbury. It opens you up to the immensity of who you really are, and reveals the hidden, sacred parts of yourself that, burdened by daily life, are usually ignored. Its power is accessible to everyone, of all faiths or none. It is a connection to spirit that goes beyond religion to the very heart of belief – be that in God, goddess or the purity of nature – and the universal energy that links all things.

Being in Glastonbury will awaken the magic of Avalon within you. As you sit at the Well, drink its healing waters, gaze at its peaceful gardens, climb the Tor and watch the moon rise or the sun set, perform sacred rituals, reflect on the history and the myths, absorb the power and beauty of the place, and the old wisdom in the trees, the hills, the wind and the stars, you'll integrate the magic that is so intrinsically linked to this ancient town – and realise that it's within your heart too, no matter where you live or what you do.

The psychic connection

Quick tips to integrate the wisdom of Glastonbury and Avalon

1. Read *The Mists of Avalon* by Marion Zimmer Bradley, which will touch your heart and help unleash your inner priestess. Since it was first published in 1983 it's inspired thousands of people to visit Glastonbury and learn more about the area's magic, or embrace its power from home. While considered a work of fiction, the book is firmly rooted in reality. Marion studied the writings of Dion Fortune, researched magic with modern-day witch Starhawk, and spent time with local tour guide Jamie George to learn the history and myths of Avalon. There's also a beautiful telemovie based on the book, and several sequels and prequels that also weave the stories of Avalon within them.

2. Open up to the faery realm. Paint, draw, write about or hang pictures of the magical winged beings that live in the mist-shrouded dimension of Avalon. Morgen la Fey was reputedly half faery, and even today it's not hard to imagine these mythical creatures flitting through the ancient trees of Glastonbury. The magic and beauty of the archetypal energy of the fae will stir something deep within you and touch your heart, bringing joy and inspiration, while their vibration can alter yours and bring lightness to your soul. Within the old faerytales there are also hidden truths (and fun!), so channel your inner faery.

3. Meditate on pictures of the Chalice Well Gardens, and let their magic change you. I don't understand how, but just seeing photos of this place has healed people of serious illnesses, without them having to be there physically. There are beautiful images on the website, www.chalicewell.org.uk, where you can buy paintings, cards and books inspired by the Well, the pools and the gardens, as well as exploring the links and finding out more about this sacred place.

4. In addition to drinking from the Well, which is very healing, people have used the waters of the Red and White Springs in homeopathic essences, both as a physical treatment and in spiritual rituals as a way to connect with the energies of Glastonbury and Avalon. In the Chalice Well Gardens a healing essence is made from the flowers and buds of the holy thorn tree, which helps you feel loved, discover your purpose and be supported through transformation. There's also an Essence of Avalon range, which distils the energies of the two oaks, Gog and Magog, as well as the Eggstone and the Holy Thorn, into vibrational medicines that bring healing and a connection to this powerful place. Others too have worked this magical water into remedies, and you can also buy pretty pendants from the Chalice Well shop that have a glass vial of the blessed Well water with a depiction of the vesica piscis, so you can hold the water literally close to your heart.

5. Explore a method of divination, be it scrying, dream journalling, tarot cards, angel oracles, psychometry or a pendulum, and spend at least a month recording the results so that you can start to see patterns emerging and begin to understand the personal meaning of all of the symbols you see. Becoming a professional psychic or tarot reader involves a lifetime of study, but you'll be amazed by what you can learn about yourself and how well you can develop your own abilities and connect to your intuition if you practise regularly.

The Armchair Traveller's Way to Visit

> "Herbal magic is one of the easiest, safest and most joyous methods of re-establishing earth roots and of returning to a healthy and natural life. It touches the essence of life itself, and is a co-operation between plant and human, earth and heaven, a union of energies forged to produce change by methods that outsiders view as supernatural."
>
> *Scott Cunningham, US author and natural magic practitioner*

The energy of Glastonbury – and Avalon – awakens the powers you have within you and allows you to see yourself as a magical being connected to the universe and to the past, present and future. While being there physically will nurture you as you explore your inner wisdom, you can also achieve this quest at home. If you feel drawn to Glastonbury but can't make your own journey to the town to gaze into the waters of Chalice Well or sit on top of the Tor, there are still many ways you can embrace the eternal magic of this beautiful place.

One method is to channel the wisdom of the priestesses and druids who lived there peacefully for so long. They were the doctors and spiritual advisers of their communities – they healed the sick, helped women give birth, counselled the depressed, divined the future, brewed love potions, warded off evil, led the rituals to bless the crops, settled disputes, performed marriage and baby naming ceremonies, helped people face death and presided over funeral rites.

You can connect to this ancient wisdom by studying herbcraft, which is the basis of all magical systems. Learning about the medicinal and magical properties of herbs, and how to not only heal people of physical ailments but also to help with spiritual matters such as protection, love, working through grief and drawing love and abundance into their lives, will fill you with the energy of Avalon.

Herbal medicine is the oldest form of health care, and has been practised in cultures throughout the world for as long as history has been recorded. Thousands of years ago physicians from as far afield as Egypt, China, Rome and India used the therapeutic properties of herbs to heal the sick, and they're also mentioned in *The Bible*.

Today eighty per cent of the earth's population still uses herbs as a major source of health care, and even in the west, where it has long been discouraged and dismissed as folk superstition, herbal medicine is becoming an increasingly respected healing tool.

Far from being an old-fashioned craft with no relevance today, herbs are the basis of many modern medicines. Aspirin was developed based on the compounds in the herb willow bark, which for centuries was used for pain relief and fever. Ephedrine, an ingredient in medications for asthma patients, is based on the herb ephedra, which has been used in Chinese medicine for more than two thousand years. Digoxin, the life-saving heart drug, is based on compounds in the herb foxglove. And quinine, the anti-malarial drug, is based on properties extracted from the bark of South America's cinchona tree.

There are many colleges that teach degrees in medicinal and clinical herbalism for those who want to become a practitioner and treat physical ailments with herbal remedies. There are also shorter courses and extensive reference books that introduce the basics so you can start to work with herbs for yourself. A warning though – herbs are natural, yet they are powerful healers with intense therapeutic effects, and serious medical conditions should only be diagnosed and treated by a professional. But anyone can start growing herbs and using their properties to promote health and wellbeing.

Drinking herbal teas and adding fresh plants such as parsley and basil to your food will boost vitality.

Herbal compresses, ointments, massage oils and inhalations can increase healing. And aromatherapy, skin lotions and herbal hair care products can help treat simple conditions and prevent ill health. For example, chamomile and passionflower alleviate insomnia, peppermint can be used to relieve nausea, and rosemary is a general tonic and boosts memory.

To feel the magic of the land, grow your own herbs, either in a whole garden or a single pot on a balcony or windowsill. Watching plants grow from seeds or seedlings, learning the difference between perennials and annuals and watching the seasonal shifts within your garden will attune you to nature and the cycles of the year, and connect you to the earth in a similar way to the old priestesses of Avalon.

Learning the ancient art of magical herbalism, an important priestess craft, is another way to channel this ancient wisdom. The use of herbs to create change on a spiritual and emotional level, common to all belief systems and cultures, is one of the oldest and most powerful magical methods. From the Ancient Egyptians and Greeks to Celtic priestesses and shamans of the Americas, herbs have been used in various magical ways since the dawn of time.

Herbs each have a specific therapeutic effect, and they also have spiritual and emotional properties, such as lavender being used to calm the mind and in rituals for love, cinnamon to increase psychic abilities, ginger to attract abundance and success, and bay leaves to promote courage. There are courses and encyclopaedic books both old and new that teach these magical properties, as well as how to cast spells, perform rituals, create talismans and herbal sachets and enchant your life with your own magical powers and the added boost of fresh or dried herbs.

While old legends and literal retellings of symbolic stories have given magic a reputation as being made up or Otherworldly and out of the reach of ordinary people, it's actually a natural part of life that can be utilised by everyone. Magic is an ancient path of wisdom and knowledge, the science of manifestation, which involves the directing of your own energies, intent and actions to achieve a desired outcome.

Magical herbalism adds the magical properties of herbs to your own innate powers, as well as the life force and energy of the universe to create real change in the physical world. It's still used in many indigenous cultures, and increasingly by modern practitioners, for spiritual healing, prophecy and protection, as well as to attract love, abundance, career success and happiness.

The priestesses of Avalon also practised scrying, a method of seeing the future by staring at a surface and taking note of the images and symbols on it. They gazed into the sacred waters of Chalice Well, but it can also be done using a bowl of water, a crystal ball (as the gypsies so famously do), a piece of black obsidian, a lake, a pool of ink or a mirror, which is the method famed seer Nostradamus employed.

To try it, fill a bowl with water, adding ink if you prefer, light a candle or sit outside under the moonlight, and stare into the water's surface. Clear your mind and focus solely on the water. Take note of any images you see, either here or in your mind's eye, and write them all down so you can analyse and start to interpret them later. Scrying requires lots of practise and patience, but can bring intriguing results.

If you're using a mirror or a crystal ball to scry, you can boost the effect by rubbing fresh mugwort leaves on the surface to strengthen its power. Magical herbalists also recommend drinking an infusion of mugwort tea before divination work to boost psychic abilities, and that you burn mugwort and wormwood incense while scrying.

Mugwort has long been revered as a powerful visionary herb, and in many ancient cultures the dried leaves were stuffed in dream pillows or sachets to stimulate and enhance prophetic dreaming. Remedially this herb has been used as a digestive stimulant and by women for general good health and female cycles, although it should be avoided during pregnancy and can be toxic in high doses.

Wormwood is also a visionary herb, with similar properties to mugwort. The priestesses of old believed it was sacred to the Greek goddess Artemis and her Roman counterpart Diana, as well as local deities, which is reflected in its botanical name, Artemisia absinthium, while mugwort's is Artemisia vulgaris. Remedially it's used for stomach and digestive disorders and migraines, amongst other conditions, but it has an unpleasant taste and can cause side effects if ingested in large doses or for more than a short period of time.

However you do it, developing your intuition is a powerful way to attune yourself to the energy of Glastonbury and Avalon and to increase your happiness, connect with your inner truth and improve your life.

"The festivals of the Wheel of the Year are defined by the cycle of nature, by the dance of the weather gods and spirits of place. They require us to look not to the heavens but to the earth. They are set within our soul, watching the leaves on the trees, feeling the shifting temperature and the changing light, within and around."

Emma Restall Orr, British druid priestess, ritualist and author

Another way to bring the magic of Glastonbury and Avalon into your life is to celebrate the eight sacred sabbats, or festivals, of the Wheel of the Year, as the ancient priestesses did – and modern pagans still do – and perform meaningful personal rituals that will inspire your own growth and the manifestation of your dreams, and bring enchantment to your daily life.

In ancient times, when life revolved around agriculture and the sun and moon were considered deities to be worshipped, the Celtic people of Britain were in tune with nature. They had to know when each season began and how long it would last so they could plant and harvest crops, hunt migratory prey and prepare for the harsh winters. They divided their year by seasons, not months, and honoured each change, celebrating eight festivals that marked the turning of these seasons and the cycles of the earth.

There were four astronomical and four agricultural festivals. The astronomical celebrations were determined by the position of the earth in relation to the sun, and included the spring and autumn equinoxes ("equinox" being Latin for equal night), which occur when the sun is directly over the equator and the length of day and night is exactly equal, and the summer and winter solstices ("solstice" being Latin for sun stand still), which occur when the sun is at its northern or southernmost extreme, the furthest it ever gets from the equator. These four events are the midpoint of each season – thus the summer solstice was known as Midsummer's Day and the winter solstice as Midwinter.

The agricultural celebrations were referred to as the cross-quarter days because they fell midway between the astronomical festivals. They were tied to agricultural events such as the sowing and harvesting of crops, and marked the beginning of each season.

The ancients were very aware of when these seasonal events occurred. They watched the sky and noted where the sun rose and set each day in its arc from north to south, and observed the behaviour of birds and animals and the growth of plants. They constructed stone circles, ritual cairns and other monuments, such as Stonehenge in England and Newgrange in Ireland, which were aligned to sunrise or sunset on one of the solstices or equinoxes. These acted as giant calendars, and alerted them to these special days and the passing of time.

Even today, when we no longer live in harmony with the earth's rhythms or agricultural cycles, modern pagans celebrate the Wheel of the Year as an honouring of nature and an acknowledgement of the continuing cycle of life, death and rebirth, both literally and symbolically. Becoming aware of the seasonal shifts and the patterns of nature wherever you live, and celebrating these ancient but still relevant festivals, is a simple way to tap in to the magic of the universe and start to develop your inner priest or priestess.

Channelling this magic and creating meaningful rituals in your life doesn't conflict with any religion or require a belief system, as it's a celebration of the science of nature and the cycles of the planet. Many pagans do call on gods and/or goddesses, and have a personal concept of the divine as a universal creative force, but others don't believe in any form of deity, simply revering nature as sacred and as the source of life, and believing that divinity is an inner not an outer power, an energy within themselves and every other person alive.

Attuning yourself to nature isn't hard – simply start paying attention to the time the sun rises and sets, the phases of the moon, and the trees in your street as they flower, lose their leaves, then start to blossom again. Walk through a park or along a beach and feel the tides of the earth and the energy of the universe as it surrounds you and moves through you. The Wheel of the Year represents the eternal cycle of life, death and rebirth. Literally this refers to the changing seasons – the fertility and vibrant life force of summer, the introspection and endings (death) of winter, and the rebirth of spring.

Mythologically this was tied to the story of the god and goddess. At the spring equinox they meet and court, before consummating their love during the rites of Beltane. At the summer solstice the goddess blooms into the mother, pregnant with new life, and the sun god reaches his energetic peak. From then he weakens through the harvest time of Lughnasadh and the autumn equinox, before going to the underworld at Samhain to learn new wisdom, then being reborn at the winter solstice when the goddess gives birth to the infant sun god and the wheel turns again, playing out the cycle on and on through time.

Back then this creation story was accepted as fact. Today there are some pagans who still believe it to be a literal retelling of a historical truth, while others feel it's simply a parable that humanises nature. Either way, it's now the symbolic meaning that's most relevant to our lives – planting the seeds of our dreams in the metaphorical spring, then watching them grow and manifest in the world before we give thanks for our literal harvest, allow the things that no longer serve us to die off or be released, then start all over again with new dreams as we celebrate our own rebirth.

The Eight Sacred Sabbats

Yule : Winter Solstice : Rebirth

The winter solstice, known to pagans as Yule, falls on December 21 or 22 in the northern hemisphere and June 21 or 22 in the south. It's the shortest day and the longest night of the year, and marks the transition between dark and light, both emotionally and physically. It's the lowest point of the Wheel of the Year in terms of daylight and energy. The land is barren, cold and infertile, there is less light than ever, and energetically people feel tired and unmotivated.

Winter is a time to rest and reflect, to acknowledge sadness and loss – of dreams, of friendships, of parts of your self – and conserve your energy and life force. Doctors have recently discovered that the long darkness of winter can cause depression, with Seasonal Affective Disorder now a recognised medical condition, so don't be hard on yourself if you suffer a touch of the winter blues – sunlight affects brain chemistry, and its lack can impact on your wellbeing.

But the solstice is the turning point in this time of darkness, introspection and dreaming. Considered the dark night of the soul, which gives birth to the creative spark, it marks the period when the dark half of the year relinquishes its hold to the light half. From this day forward the days will slowly start to lengthen, the sun will become stronger and the energy within and without will increase and build.

In pagan times an evergreen tree was brought inside on this night as a symbol of the hope of spring's return, and Yule was a time of feasting, celebration and gift giving in honour of the birth of the sun god – traditions that live on today in the Christmas tree that's decorated at this time, the presents we put under it, the huge family meals we cook and the recognition of the birth of the son of God.

To attune yourself to the Wheel of the Year and this festival of hope and renewal, light a candle on solstice eve to symbolise the sun and its activating energy, and list your dreams for the coming year. Traditionally people stayed up all night to await the return of the light, but if you can't do that, get up for the sunrise to toast the dawn and give thanks for this energetic reawakening.

Open yourself to the promise of new growth and achievement, the rebirth of your own self and your creativity as the sun is also reborn. Symbolically and energetically it's a time to honour your inner wisdom, consider the lessons you learned during winter's introspection and integrate them into your life so you can start to initiate change.

In Glastonbury there is a small ceremony at the Chalice Well Gardens to mark this solstice each year, in gardens that are often snow-covered and so still, just perfect for this season of introspection and energy withdrawal. The Goddess Temple also holds a beautiful fire ritual to mark the Midwinter and the rebirth of the sun.

Imbolc: First Day of Spring: Purification

Imbolc, celebrated in the first week of February in the northern hemisphere and the first week of August in the south, is a cross-quarter day marking the end of winter, which celebrates the return of light to the land. It's a time of hope, renewal and fresh starts after winter's sluggishness, and is the first of three fertility festivals.

Imbolc comes from the Irish word for ewe's milk, and is sometimes translated as in the belly, because sheep were pregnant at this time, swelling with new life. The first signs of winter's end appear, the first tentative flowers bloom and the sun strengthens, symbolising the return and renewal of the life force of the land and its people, and the coming of spring.

Energetically it's a time of awakening and new energy, and is the day to sow the seeds of what you want to achieve in the coming year. It's dedicated to Bridie, the goddess of inspiration, creativity and fire, who was later supplanted by Saint Bridget, whose festival is now celebrated at this time. Talk to Bridie – or Bridget or the higher self aspect of yourself – or write her a letter, and tell her what you want to create in the next twelve months. Meditate on your goals and what you hope to achieve. Don't worry about how to do it, as that will be revealed later as flashes of inspiration, guidance or outside help.

This is a time of purification and cleansing after the long dark of winter, so clean your house and energetically clear your space, sweeping out old energy and thoughts so the new can thrive. You can also light a candle to represent the coming back of the light, and do some candle magic. Stare into the flame as you concentrate on what you want, then blow it out, sending your desire out to the universe. Making a wish as you blow out the candles on your birthday cake is a magic that has survived from pagan times, and is a potent way to manifest your wishes into reality, whatever day it is.

In Glastonbury at this time there is a ceremony at Chalice Well Gardens to mark the First Stirring, as spring makes its first tentative return, while the Goddess Temple and its priestesses hold a ritual dedicated to the goddess Bridie and the maiden aspect of the Great Mother.

Ostara : Spring Equinox : Blossoming

The spring or vernal equinox, known to witches and pagans as Ostara, is celebrated on March 20 or 21 in the northern hemisphere and September 22 or 23 in the south. It's one of only two times each year that the length of day and night is exactly equal, as the sun sits directly above the equator on its journey north or south, creating equal light and dark in both hemispheres.

On a personal level it's a time of balance and harmony, of union between the physical and spiritual, which can be harnessed to anchor your dreams in reality and enhance your own inner harmony as the balance of universal energies is reflected within. Relationships are harmonious too, making it a good time for weddings and for healing rifts.

It's also a time of growth and fertility, when new crops are sown, new shoots break through the earth, buds on the trees open, birds build nests and lay eggs and new life is celebrated. Thanks was traditionally given to the fertility goddess Ostara, whose symbols were an egg and a hare, and who is still honoured around the world today, albeit unknowingly, in the form of chocolate eggs and the Easter bunny.

Energetically it's also a very fertile time, as the seeds you previously sowed of your goals begin to sprout and gain momentum. Paint some hard-boiled eggs or buy or make the chocolate version, meditating on your own metaphorical fertility and your ability to manifest dreams into reality. Choose an affirmation relating to your desired outcome, write it down and pin it up where you'll be able to see it every day.

Go outside during the day and breathe in the fresh spring air, filling your heart with new inspiration as you fill your lungs with oxygen. In many ancient cultures, including the Romans whose calendar ours is based on, the spring equinox was the first day of the year, and the sense of new hope and optimism reflected in this time remains today. It's a celebration of new life, hope, passion, growth and revitalising energy.

In Glastonbury, the equinox is marked each year with a ceremony at Chalice Well Gardens, as well as beautiful rituals in the Goddess Temple.

Beltane : First Day of Summer : Growth

Beltane, celebrated in early May in the northern hemisphere and early November in the south, is a cross-quarter day marking the end of spring and the start of the heat and energy of summer. The evidence of new life is everywhere, in abundant blossoms, the hatching of birds, and bees pollinating flowers, proving that time is moving forward and life is progressing along its path. Women would bathe their faces in the dew gathered from their garden on Beltane morning to harness the energy of youth, and flowers were brought inside to symbolise fresh beginnings and the power of nature.

Beltane was the major fertility festival, and lovers leaped over bonfires hand in hand to renew their vows of love, then came together in sacred union in the fields to bless the crops with fertility. Maypole dancing, representing the union of the god (the pole) and the goddess (the ribbons), joined the two forces of masculine and feminine, and May Day was – and still is – one of the most popular days for marriages in the northern hemisphere. It's a time of lovers and spells to attract love, and celebrating the fertility of life, not just physically, but also of your dreams and ambitions.

Symbolically this day marks the igniting of the fires of creativity and passion, of the power of your dreams being made manifest, and is the perfect time to take positive steps to achieve what you most want. Magic can enhance and help you achieve your goals, but you still need to put the physical effort in. The energy of this day will support you as you take action. Start a new project, apply for a new job or take up a new hobby, knowing the universe is bursting with raw energy and power that you can tap in to simply by breathing it in.

It's also a powerful time to repledge your love to your partner. You don't have to build a bonfire and leap over it (although you can!). Simply lighting a red or gold candle as you stare into each other's eyes and speak your love and commitment is enough to invoke the power and passion of the element of fire. If you're single, make a commitment of some kind to yourself, such as achieving a goal or starting a new project, nurture a friendship, or sing your intention and your wanting of a romantic partner to the universe.

Beltane is a big time for celebration in Glastonbury, with lots of rituals to welcome summer and symbolise the fertility of the season. At Chalice Well Gardens they hold their Mayday Ceremony, to honour the energy of Flowering, and often have a Well dressing event just before it, then a Beltane fire ritual at dawn, where you can leap over the fire and symbolically burn off whatever you no longer want to hold on to. There are also beautiful rituals at the Goddess Temple at this time, focusing on love and fertility, both literal and metaphorical.

Litha : Summer Solstice : Fruition

The summer solstice, known as Litha, is celebrated on June 20 or 21 in the northern hemisphere and December 21 or 22 in the south. It's the longest day and the shortest night of the year, and marks the peak of energy and solar power for the year. On this day the sun reaches its northern or southernmost latitude before it turns and heads back towards the equator, so near the poles daylight lasts for 24 hours. Everything is ripe and abundant and life is blooming.

Universally it's a time of high, hot and active energy. Creativity and expression is at a peak, so stand in your power and express your needs, saying what you want rather than assuming people know. Whereas the winter solstice is slow and introspective, its opposite is fast and effective. Make use of the active energy – this is a time to do, to get out there and harness the energising power and make things happen. It's also a time when relationships – and you – will mature, and you'll be able to apply new wisdom and forethought to your passion.

It's a time of celebration too, of acknowledging how far you've come and what you've achieved. Enjoy the happiness and abundance of this season and soak up the sunshine and festive atmosphere. Traditionally people stayed up all night on solstice eve, partying around the bonfires or within the sacred circles, then watched the sun rise the next morning, feeling it bathe them in warmth and light.

At dawn, stand with your arms outstretched and breathe in the sun's life-giving powers. Let these golden rays wash over you with their healing energy and burn away anything you no longer need. Take note of how your dreams and goals are progressing, and meditate on anything that could be blocking your progress. Be open to letting go of whatever isn't working so you can move forward in a new direction.

In Glastonbury at this time there are many celebrations, as people take advantage of the long days and the beautiful weather. Many climb the Tor at sunset, or after the Midsummer Night's Eve ritual in the Chalice Well Gardens, and stay up there throughout this shortest night, singing, playing music, meditating and waiting to see the beautiful Midsummer sun rise over the mists of Avalon and light up the world. I must admit though, it gets pretty chilly up there at 3am, so take extra layers if you venture to the summit. The Goddess Temple also holds a beautiful, meaningful ritual.

Lughnasadh:
First Day of Autumn: Gratitude

Lughnasadh, or Lammas, celebrated in the first week of August in the northern hemisphere and the first week of February in the south, is a cross-quarter day marking the end of summer and the beginning of autumn. It's the first harvest festival, traditionally a time of feasting and of thanksgiving for the life-giving properties of the grain, as well as a recognition of the cycle of sowing and reaping of the crops – and of the symbolic things you grow and create in your life.

It's a day of harvesting the fruits of your labours and acknowledging your successes and what you've achieved in the past year. Celebrate the goals you've reached and have your own festival of gratitude, in whatever form that takes. Toast your success, throw a party or do something special to mark the occasion. Make a list of all the things you've gained over the past year – the gifts you've been given, the new talents you've developed, the friends you've made, the experiences you've had, the healings you've received – and give thanks for it all.

Then, out of gratitude and in the spirit of the ancestors who shared the bounty of their harvest with those less well off, pass on some of your good fortune. Make a donation to a local charity, lend money to a business in the developing world or give your time to help someone, ensuring the energy of abundance continues and is strengthened. Give out of grace and for joy, not with the expectation of receiving anything in return. Work out small ways you can make a difference to the world and the people around you all year.

Now too, as the energy begins to subtly slow, it's a time to be patient and to trust that everything is as it should be, because there are still harvests to come. Not everything has to be achieved right now – some things take longer to manifest. The lesson of the Wheel of the Year is that everything continues, everything happens when it should, and everything is eternal.

If you are in Glastonbury at this time you can take part in the annual Goddess Conference, which runs for more than a week and is dedicated to a different goddess each time. It includes powerful circles, wonderful workshops by international spiritual teachers and rituals run by the priestesses of Avalon, all of which you can take part in, plus performances, offerings, crafting, art exhibitions, social events and much more, at venues all over Glastonbury. Visit www.goddessconference.com for information, inspiration and bookings.

Mabon : Autumn Equinox : Harvest

The autumn equinox, known as Mabon and celebrated on September 22 or 23 in the northern hemisphere and March 20 or 21 in the south, is characterised, like the spring equinox, by the length of day and night being equal as the sun travels back across the equator to the other hemisphere. From this point on the days will become shorter and the weather will get cooler, but today is the moment of balance in nature and within – a time of harmony and gentle calm.

Mabon is the time to honour your achievements, experiences and wisdom, and to ensure balance in your life by integrating all the parts of your self. On this day, when all is balanced, witches traditionally renewed their magical commitments, and you can renew any vows you've made or pledge a new one, be it to do with magic, love, friendship, career or anything else. It's also a harvest festival, a time to further celebrate your achievements and feel fulfilment from each one, releasing what no longer serves you in order to move forward. In the wild, old growth is cleared. In your life, cut out anything that's holding you back, draining you or preventing new life and love from flourishing, whether it's work, people, a belief system, regret or the past.

As the shadows lengthen, it's also a good time to scry if you want insight into your future. If you can, light a fire and stare into the flames, allowing your mind to go blank and your vision to blur a little. Note any images you see. Or go outside and watch the clouds scuttling across the sky and analyse the shapes you see within them. Without thinking about it too much, write down what they mean to you.

Pyromancy (fire reading) and nephomancy (cloud reading) are forms of divination that have been used for millennia. You should eventually develop your own dictionary of symbols, because you know better than anyone else what each symbol means to you, but you can begin with standard readings, such as a heart indicating new romance, a cat referring to the need to trust your intuition, a tree meaning you'll make new friends and a plane foreshadowing travel.

In Glastonbury, there is an Autumn Equinox ceremony at Chalice Well Gardens each year, which usually includes a meditation in this beautiful place, while the Goddess Temple and its priestesses also celebrate this turning of the Wheel of the Year.

Samhain : First Day of Winter : Death

Samhain, celebrated in early November in the northern hemisphere and early May in the south – and in popular culture on October 31 – is a cross-quarter day marking the end of autumn and the beginning of the coldness and dark of winter. Long ago, food had to be stored at this time for the cold barren months ahead, when snow covered the land and fresh food was scarce. Animals, who could no longer find grass for grazing, were slaughtered and preserved for later eating.

Symbolically this festival is about rest and renewal, of preparing for what's ahead and withdrawing a little to conserve your energy. It's also the night when the veil between the worlds is at its thinnest, and people traditionally honoured their ancestors and tried to commune with the dead. Some simply set an extra place at the dinner table for a relative who'd passed over, while others cast spells to bring their spirit back to the land of the living, or did mediumship rituals to converse. This magical time and its purpose has been conserved in the modern-day festival of Halloween, which celebrates ghosts and witches, and the Christian holidays of All Hallow's Eve and All Saints Day.

It's a period of inner reflection, so spend time in quiet contemplation. If you've lost someone close to you, light a candle and remember them. Look at photos or letters and feel their presence with you. It shouldn't be morbid – you're celebrating their life and all they meant to you. Also honour those who *are* here. Call your mum and dad, visit your grandparents, write to someone who meant a lot to you when you were growing up and thank them for the moments they shared with you.

In ancient times, Samhain was the end of one year and the beginning of the next, so it's also a powerful time to let go of the energy of the old year and old memories so you can move forward with lightness and strength. Light another candle and, by its flickering illumination, write out all the worries, frustrations, regrets and seeming failures you've held on to over the past twelve months. See the candle flame burning them away and leaving you purified and refreshed, and breathe in this positive new energy. Then burn the list in the flame, releasing your attachment to those emotions and their power over you.

This is the time to prepare yourself for the rebirth you'll experience at Yule, but for that to happen there must be death – the death of your fears and doubts, and anything that's holding you back.

In Glastonbury at this time of year there are beautiful ceremonies in the Goddess Temple, honouring the goddess in her aspect as crone, with temple dressing events in the days leading up to it, while at Chalice Well Gardens they have an All Hallow's Eve ritual to mark this time of Resting, which usually includes fancy dress, hot pumpkin soup and activities for the young and the young at heart.

The Wheel of the Year

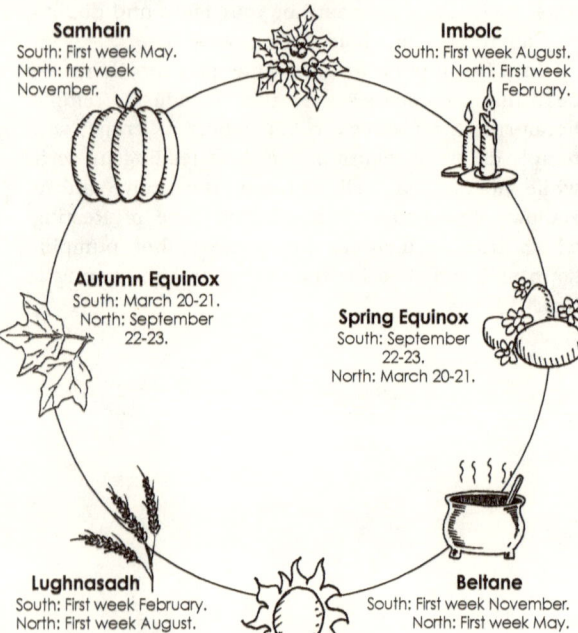

Postcard from Glastonbury

Colette Baron-Reid is a Canadian-born intuitive counsellor and the author of *Remembering the Future: The Path to Recovering Intuition* and *Messages From Spirit: The Extraordinary Power of Oracles, Omens and Signs*, which recount her own spiritual journey and include exercises to develop your psychic powers.

She tours alone and with American psychic Sylvia Browne, teaching seminars and giving audience readings. She is also a singer, and has released two albums of her songs in addition to the meditation CD *Journey Through the Chakras*.

Colette is now based in Sedona, USA, but has visited the magical town of Glastonbury a few times, and feels a strong past life link to it. She created *The Wisdom of Avalon Oracle Cards* to help other people connect to the energy that can be accessed in this sacred place. Visit www.colettebaronreid.net.

My connection to Glastonbury goes back a long time. When I was in kindergarten I would draw a blue crescent moon on my forehead whenever I had paints. Fast forward to my late twenties, when I first read *The Mists of Avalon* in the late 80s, and I was struck dumb by the description of the blue crescent moons tattooed on the foreheads of the priestesses, because I had such a strong memory of having done that as a kid. The story felt very familiar to me too. Not so much that I knew King Arthur, but the description of the forest, the mists and their methods of divination and scrying were so vivid to me.

Ten years after that I went to Glastonbury for the first time, but I went with a group of people, which was very distracting, and I felt really disjointed. But the land was calling me. It was a very strong magnetic pull to my psyche, and I felt this strange sense of longing and yearning, so later I went back on my own, and that was when I felt I'd come home. I could feel a presence there, something that grew around me, that beckoned to me, that was very much alive. And I heard whispers and saw buildings out of the corner of my eye that weren't there when I looked directly, but had been in the past.

My most incredible experience was at the Chalice Well Gardens. As I walked towards the Well, all of a sudden it became like a place I'd been to before, and I recognised it from a vision I'd had a few months earlier. I'd been learning reiki, but during the attunement I found myself in another dimension. My jeans became a rough scratchy dress, I smelled different, I was aware I hadn't shaved my legs, and I was suddenly in a circle around a well being initiated by a different group of women. I saw deerskins, so I thought it was a Native American past life, but then I noticed the blue moons on the women's foreheads.

So now as I was walking towards Chalice Well I was in shock, because all of a sudden I was those two women again, me in the now and me from another life, the one I'd seen before. My sense of location became altered and I felt a merging of energy inside me. I was very aware that I was in two places at once – that I was the person I am now, a Christian woman, but that I was equally a priestess worshipping the goddess around the Well. It was strange, because in the physical present world it was raining, but the other me could see through the branches above that it was sunny in the other life.

It was as though I was straddling two entire worlds, and nature was allowing me to witness myself in the two dimensions. I started to cry, and for a brief instant I had access to this well of knowledge from this other life, a clear sense of memory. It faded as I walked away, but at that moment all of it was available to me.

Chalice Well Gardens is my favourite place in Glastonbury, because I've had incredible experiences there which confirmed for me that my path as an intuitive is the right one, but I also like to walk up the Tor, and I like sitting inside the tower at the top on my own, because from up there you can see what it would have been like back then.

Many people have visions of the past and the future when they are in Glastonbury because the leyline energy makes the veils between the worlds so thin there. I can't really explain leylines, I just know that they are there, I know that they pull you. You can feel their power physically, viscerally.

I felt as though I was an instrument someone was playing when I was there – I really felt that I had strings. It's almost overwhelming sometimes, and you can feel a little dizzy until you adjust to the energy. But the leylines help you feel things, and if you allow your senses to open you'll have a very strong amplified sensory experience while you're there.

The wisdom of Avalon is attached to the land, so when you go to Glastonbury today you can connect to it. Anyone can go there and ask for visions and they will come. I believe you can access this wisdom from anywhere, but you will definitely have a much bigger experience if you go there, because the physical place is very important.

Spending time in Glastonbury reminds me of something, because the spirit of Avalon has never left it. I live in the city, I get caught up in my busy life and the memory fades, but being in Glastonbury opens my awareness to the deeper levels. It makes the lost sense of spirituality accessible again so I remember what is most important in life. A visit to Glastonbury also helps people to remember the sacred quality of nature and inspires a vision of eco-spirituality, which we need today for our own survival.

Postcard from Avalon

Lucy Cavendish is an Australian witch who embraces magic as a belief system of personal fulfilment and happiness. She is the author of *White Magic, Witches and Wizards, Magickal Faerytales, Spellbound* and *The Lost Lands*, and creator of *The Oracle Tarot, The Wild Wisdom of the Faery Oracle, Magical Spell Cards, The Oracle of Shadows & Light, Oracle of the Dragonfae* and many more. She is a writer, ritualist and psychic, and has released the space clearing CD *As Above So Below* and the guided meditation *Return to Avalon*, as well as hosting The Witchcast podcast.

Lucy feels deeply connected to Avalon, and facilitates workshops that impart the wisdom and teachings of the druids and priestesses of the sacred isle. She took her first spiritual group to England in 2010, to explore Somerset, Wiltshire and Cornwall, and plans many more such magical pilgrimages. Visit www.lucycavendish.com.au.

While the geophysical location of Avalon is in the town of Glastonbury in England, there is also an Avalon of the heart, a world between the worlds that we all carry within us, and which I believe can be tapped in to from anywhere on the planet.

I first reached Avalon long before I travelled to Glastonbury. As a child I went there in dreams, and when I began practising magic I accessed this in-between world during ritual, spellcasting and chanting. Avalon is a sacred space between the worlds that is within all of us. It is another dimension where we can get in touch with our inner world, as well as the Otherworld where all knowledge resides.

Avalon is a sacred joining of the elements, our own faery self, and our connection to the highest principles of love and service, romance and magic. It's a mystical state we can go to through meditation, by communicating with the goddess or by invoking it in ritual.

In my workshops I guide people through a series of magical processes that connect them with the ancient crafts of the Avalonian priestesses and activate their psychic abilities, but you can do this yourself if you open your heart to the wisdom and purity of Avalon.

It is easier to access at the special times of the year – the enchanted sabbat nights when the veils between this world and the Other are thinner and we can communicate with spirits and elementals – but it can be reached at any time, through the power of thought and intention. Avalon can also be accessed when you invoke the goddesses of the place – Bridie, Rhiannon and Ceridwen – as well as Morgen la Fey and Guinevere, the goddess who still remains to be reclaimed. She is no tragic victim – she is a true goddess of the land, and she wants us to find her and know her again.

Many of us can also access Avalon easily because we had past lives there, so we have a strong cellular memory of it. I feel the magnetic pull of several lifetimes there, where I lived and worked as part of a sacred community. Avalon is the place where we become one with our spirit, where we can achieve great healing, see the future and manifest what we need and want.

Being in Avalon healed a part of me that was wounded. Its compassion is limitless and its teachings are endless. Avalon is a dimension and an experience that can bring women and men into their power in a way that creates love and respect for the earth plane, for our beautiful planet, for our bodies and for our relationships. Avalon heals everyone, but our individual experience of her will differ according to our own unique vibrational blueprint.

It is linked to modern witchcraft because it includes the teachings of the druids and priestesses of the Celtic world, and learning to hear the voice of the earth mother. It is the belief that everything is sacred, that we are a part of nature and must respect and protect it, and that the earth is alive and connected to us. It gives us a vision of a life lived in harmony with the ancient wisdom that is in tune with the planet.

Visiting the dimension of Avalon will impart to you the teachings of the druids and priestesses of the Celtic world and the sacred rites that help us to hear and feel, see and know the voice, the face, the wisdom and the knowledge of the earth mother. It also includes the teachings of Atlantis and Lemuria that survived in the apple groves, the significance of the apple – the element of Avalon that has remnants in the story of Eden and Eve – the Merlin Taliesin's sacred poetry, and connecting to the faery and elfin realms. You'll experience the difference between the "real" world that we physically live in, and Avalon – the heart place.

Dwelling so long in the dimension of Avalon, I felt a magnetic pull to visit Glastonbury, its earth plane location, and I finally went there at Beltane in 2005. How amazing it was, that I could feel so naturally at perfect ease in a place I'd never physically been. The actual landscape has true magic in it, and the water from the Well has an incredible repository of blessings within its structure that work on a physical and energetic level. Being there validated that my path, my mist-filled dreaming, is legitimate, but it also confirmed for me that the magic of Avalon is available to all, no matter where in the world you live.

Visiting this dimension today, from wherever you are, will give you access to the ancient wisdom for a more meaningful, psychically aware and healed present and future. Avalon activates your magical talents, brings a new level of awareness and purpose to all you do, and makes the everyday world enchanted and sacred. It's time to re-learn and reactivate its magic, and incorporate it within your heart and soul.

Information and inspiration

Here are a few of the books, websites, organisations, people and things that may help you find the magic on your own adventure to Glastonbury and Avalon.

One of the most enchanting places in Glastonbury is the Chalice Well Gardens. You can visit the sanctuary for a few hours or all day, stay in the cottage in the grounds with 24-hour access to the gardens, and become a Companion and support their work. Their site features information, workshop and retreats details, links, an events list and beautiful photos, with a link to their shop for lovely cards, jewellery, gifts, books and Chalice Well essences: www.chalicewell.org.uk.

The first time I stayed in Glastonbury there was a cafe and shop in the building over the White Spring, opposite Chalice Well Gardens, with the sacred water running across the floor beneath your table. It closed down a while ago, but recently a group began work to conserve the spring and its surrounds, and they now hold rituals there again: www.whitespring.org.uk.

For articles, information, photos, links, inspiration and a uniquely local perspective on the town, visit the Isle of Avalon website, a portal into the physical town as well as the etheric dimension of Avalon, and many of the sacred sites in the surrounding landscape, including Burrowbridge Mump (the baby Tor), Cadbury Castle, reputed to be the site of Camelot, and the Stanton Drew stone circles near Bristol: www.isleofavalon.co.uk.

For practical details visit the Glastonbury Tourist Information Centre: www.glastonburytic.co.uk, which is located in a beautiful old building on the High Street.

For a huge range of accommodation options, from sweet B&Bs and self-catering cottages to the local hostel: www.glastonbury.co.uk/accommodation.

Visit the Glastonbury Oracle website to find out what's on in the town right now, and several months in advance: www.glastonburyoracle.co.uk, and the Online Guide to Glastonbury: www.glastonbury.co.uk.

Journey to the Glastonbury Goddess Temple, find details of their ceremonies and rituals, download their newsletter, read about the new priestesses of Avalon and how to become one, and buy beautiful books, gifts and CDs from their shop: www.goddesstemple.co.uk.

Visit British priestess Kathy Jones at her online home to learn about her priestess training courses, order her magical books, read a free e-book, and find out about the goddess tours she leads around the world and her annual Goddess Conference: www.kathyjones.co.uk.

For information on the modern druids, visit the Order of Bards, Ovates and Druids: www.druidry.org, which has links to international member groups, and the Druid Network: www.druidnetwork.org, a group formed by druid priestess Emma Restall Orr. In Australia, Pagan Awareness Network: www.paganawareness.net.au.

For tours of the sacred places of the town led by Jamie George, as well as sacred travel around Ireland, Scotland and Cornwall, visit Gothic Image Tours: www.gothicimagetours.co.uk, and for wonderful sacred tours of the town and the British Isles in the footsteps of druids, saints and King Arthur led by Tor Webster, visit www.torstoursofthetor.com.

For Glastonbury Abbey information, pictures, history and opening details: www.glastonburyabbey.com, and for info on Saint John's Church on the High Street: www.stjohns-glastonbury.org.uk.

Glastonbury Conservation Society is involved in projects such as tree planting and improving pathways to prevent erosion of the Tor, and volunteers are always welcome. They also have a newsletter and informative articles: web.ukonline.co.uk/jim.nagel/ap/consoc.

For tourist information for Somerset County, including Cheddar Gorge, Exmoor Owl & Hawk Centre, Bishop's Palace, Avalon Vineyard and the Wookey Hole Cave, home of the Witch of Wookey: www.visitsomerset.co.uk.

Great books: *The Mists of Avalon* by Marion Zimmer Bradley is a melding of fact and fiction about the priestesses of Avalon and the connection to nature that continues to be experienced by those who visit today. *In the Nature of Avalon: Goddess Pilgrimages in Glastonbury's Sacred Landscape* by Kathy Jones outlines pilgrimage paths that weave between Avalon's sacred sites, and places the goddesses of the land into physical context. *Glastonbury: Maker of Myths* by Frances Howard-Gordon, *The Isle of Avalon* by Nicholas Mann, *New Light on the Ancient Mystery of Glastonbury* by John Michell, *King Arthur's Avalon* by Geoffrey Ashe and *The Avalonians* by Patrick Benham also deepen your insight into the area.

Great art: I have a framed print of John Shannon's Lady Avalon, which enchants me with the magic of Avalon and the priestesses of old: www.jeshannon.com. One of my favourite images of Glastonbury is Chalice Well Deva by Georgia Lambert. See her art, and hear audio lectures and spiritual teachings: www.lambertslodge.com, and buy the Chalice Well Deva greeting card from the Chalice Well shop, as she donated all reproduction rights to the trust. I also have several of artist Selina Fenech's enchanting paintings in my office, including Lady of Avalon, and they lift my heart whenever I look at them, and help unlock the wisdom I have within me, inspiring me to connect to my own self and write my truths. Check out her beautiful art at www.selinafenech.com.

Notes

Notes

☽ ○ ☾ *Notes* ☽ ○ ☾

☽○☾ *Notes* ☽○☾

Notes

Notes

Seven Sacred Sites

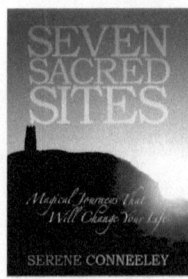

Glastonbury is one of the seven places in *Seven Sacred Sites: Magical Journeys That Will Change Your Life* (Blessed Bee Books).

In *Seven Sacred Sites*, follow the author as she awakens to the divine in Machu Picchu and the jungles of the Amazon in Peru, goes beyond the mists in Glastonbury, the magical Isle of Avalon, to reconnect with her own enchanted self, witnesses the masculine and feminine face of the divine in Ancient Egypt's mystical pyramids and temples, walks the pilgrimage path of the Camino in Spain on a journey towards her inner self, experiences the pure joy of the dolphins, rainbows and goddesses in the powerful earth energies of Hawaii, feels the wisdom within the megaliths of Stonehenge, and finds a sense of place at Uluru, the spiritual heart of Australia.

Discover what makes these places sacred, when to go and how to get there, the history and the rituals that were performed there, their cultural and magical significance, and the way they inspire, touch and initiate growth in all visitors. Just as importantly, find out how to attain the state of grace and sacredness inspired by each one without leaving home.

Including postcards from spiritual teachers and authors Cassandra Eason, Shirley MacLaine, Doreen Virtue, Lucy Cavendish, Colette Baron-Reid, Elisabeth Jensen, Jude Currivan and Alberto Villoldo, this book is part spiritual adventure story, part history, part travel guide. It will send you on a journey to the most beautiful places on the planet as well as the deepest, most sacred places within your self, and open you up to the magic of the universe, within and without.

Reviews of Seven Sacred Sites

"Sometimes, if you're lucky enough, you will come across a book that has an energy so great that it moves beyond its pages. *Seven Sacred Sites* is such a book. Brilliantly written and stunningly produced, the magical journeys within it will inspire you to dream, to travel, and to ponder your own place here on our wonderful planet."

Kylie Matthews, Manly Daily book reviewer

"*Seven Sacred Sites* is a must-read. This spiritual, historical and geographical journey will help you discover not only about our wondrous surroundings but, perhaps more importantly, yourself as well."

Andrea Black, travel editor, New Idea magazine

"This is by far the best travel book I've read this year. Conneeley's style evokes the great travel writers like Michener, who weave cultural anthropology seamlessly into an entertaining traveller's tale – a recipe for pure reading pleasure. I'd recommend this book to any armchair traveller – and it is absolute gold for those interested in the spiritual traditions that shape our world."

Joanne Lock, travel editor, Spheres magazine

"*Seven Sacred Sites* is essential reading for all those contemplating attending, or preparing for, a spiritual journey... or simply trying to understand the effect these sacred power sites have on us all."

Elisabeth Jensen, founder of Isis Mystery School

About the Author

Serene Conneeley is an Australian writer with a fascination for history, travel, ritual and the myth and magic of ancient places and cultures. She's written for magazines about news, travel, health, spirituality, entertainment, and social and environmental issues, been editor of several preschool magazines, and contributed to international books on history, witchcraft, psychic development and personal transformation.

She's the author of the original Australian faery tale *The Swan Maiden*, the Into the Mists Trilogy – *Into the Mists, Into the Dark* and *Into the Light* – the Into the Storm Trilogy – *Into the Storm, Into the Fire* and *Into the Air* – and the non-fiction books *Faery Magic, Mermaid Magic, Witchy Magic, Seven Sacred Sites* and *A Magical Journey,* and creator of the meditation CD *Sacred Journey*.

Serene is a reconnective healing practitioner, and has studied magical and medicinal herbalism, reiki, bereavement counselling and many other healing modalities, plus politics and journalism. She loves reading books, drinking tea with her friends, working out, and celebrating the energy of the moon and the magic of the earth. Her pagan heart blossomed as she climbed mountains, sat in stone circles, crawled into ancient burial mounds and stood in the shadow of the pyramids on her travels, and she's also learned the magic of finding happiness and peace at home.

www.SereneConneeley.com

Thank You

Thank you so much for reading this book.
If you enjoyed it, I would be so grateful if you could
take a moment to leave a review on any book site.
Reviews help improve sales and ranking,
and are of immense help to all indie writers.
Even a single sentence will make a difference.

If you'd like to stay in touch and receive free
exclusive content, be the first to hear about book
news, events info and giveaways, win prizes and
more, you can sign up for my newsletter at

www.sereneconneeley.com/subscribe.

(And don't worry, you can unsubscribe at any time...)

With love and gratitude,
Serene xx

Other Books By Serene

The Australian Faery Tale Series

The Swan Maiden: An Australian Faery Tale

The Into the Mists Trilogy

Into the Mists
Into the Dark
Into the Light
Into the Mists: A Journal
The Into the Mists Trilogy Hardcover Omnibus

"I'm absolutely blown away by this series. It is beautiful from start to finish – magical, realistic, gentle, harsh, sad, joyful... I've been on a total rollercoaster ride, and am now feeling so bereft at the thought that these wonderful people will no longer be part of my life."
Kylie Matthews, reviewer

The Into the Storm Trilogy

Into the Storm
Into the Fire
Into the Air

"This series is a transformative must-read. Profound, thought-provoking and empowering, it's so immersive that the magic emanates from the pages. I loved every single second of it."

Kastie Pavlik, author

The Magic Series (with Lucy Cavendish)

The Book of Faery Magic

Mermaid Magic: Connecting With the Energy of the Ocean and the Healing Power of Water

Witchy Magic

"Mermaid Magic is a wonderfully inspiring read. It made me want to shed my twenty-first century shackles and dive into the ocean to embrace its wonderful healing powers. Thank you magical ladies for the journey!"
Sabina Collins, reviewer

The Sacred Series

Seven Sacred Sites: Magical Journeys That Will Change Your Life

A Magical Journey: Your Diary of Inspiration, Adventure and Transformation

Sacred Journey: A Meditation To Connect You To the Magic of the Earth (CD)

Sacred Sites: Egypt
Sacred Sites: Glastonbury
Sacred Sites: Hawaii
Sacred Sites: Peru
Sacred Sites: Stonehenge
Sacred Sites: The Camino
Sacred Sites: Uluru

"The real voyage of discovery consists
not in seeking new landscapes,
but in having new eyes."
Marcel Proust, 20th century French writer

www.ingramcontent.com/pod-product-compliance
Lightning Source LLC
Chambersburg PA
CBHW020658300426
44112CB00007B/441